WORLD
SOCIAL STUDIES
YELLOW PAGES

FOR
STUDENTS AND TEACHERS

from
The Kids' Stuff™ People

Incentive Publications, Inc.
Nashville, Tennessee

Special acknowledgement is accorded to:
- *Sharen Lewis and Kathy LaMorte for compiling and organizing the materials included in this publication.*
- *Gayle Seaberg Harvey for the cover illustration.*
- *Rebecca Newton, editor.*

Library of Congress Catalog Card Number: 92-74236
ISBN 0-86530-268-5

TABLE OF CONTENTS

THE RISE OF CIVILIZATION
(PREHISTORY – 450 B.C.)

THE STONE AGE (2,000,000 B.C. – 8,000 B.C.)

PREHISTORIC PEOPLE
- Homo habilus
- Homo erectus
- Homo sapiens:
    - Neanderthals
    - Cro-Magnons
- Homo sapiens sapiens

KEY PLACES
- Mesopotamia
- Egypt
- Iraq

KEY TERMS
- Prehistory
- Stone Age
- New Stone Age
- Fossil
- Carbon 14 dating
- Nomad
- Ice Age
- Glacier
- Artifact
- Culture
- Migrate

LIFE-STYLE
- Hunters
- Gatherers
- Cave homes
- Animal skin clothes
- Primitive religion

KEY ACHIEVEMENTS
- Mastered fire:
    - Preserve food
    - Cook
    - Heat
    - Hunt
- Invented tools:
    - Daggers
    - Spears
    - Hand axes
    - Choppers
    - Scrapers
    - Diggers
    - Bone needles
    - Bone fishhooks
- Developed language
- Created art:
    - Jewelry
    - Sculpture
    - Pottery
    - Cave paintings

THE RISE OF CIVILIZATION (PREHISTORY—450 B.C.) *(cont.)*

THE NEW STONE AGE (8000 B.C.)

KEY EVENTS
- Agricultural revolution
- Villages formed
- Trade developed
- Domestication of animals
- Division of labor
- Specialization of skills
- Barter for goods
- Bronze Age

LIFE-STYLE
- Farmers
- Herders
- Nomads
- Artisans
- Property owners
- Woven clothing
- Brick and oak houses
- Decorated homes

KEY PLACES
- Middle East:
    - Iraq
    - Turkey
    - Egypt
- Mexico
- Thailand
- Catal Huyuk

KEY ACHIEVEMENTS
- Skilled artisans:
    - Potter's wheel
    - Basketweaving
    - Jewelry
    - Spinning/weaving
- Technology:
    - Plow
    - Wheel
    - Sail
- Harnessed animal power
- Permanent houses
- Metalworking skills

KEY TERMS
- Domesticate
- Artisan
- Barter

THE FIRST CIVILIZATIONS (3200 B.C.)

MESOPOTAMIA

KEY PEOPLE
- Sargon of Akkad
- Hammurabi

KEY EVENTS
- Establishment of city-states
- Iron Age
- Transportation
- Trade

KEY PLACES
- Mesopotamia
- Tigris-Euphrates River Valley
- Sumer
- Akkad
- Babylon
- Ur

KEY TERMS
- Civilization
- Theocracy
- City-state
- Empire
- Ziggarat
- Bazaar
- Cuneiform
- Classes

LIFE-STYLE
- Class system:
  - Ruler
  - Priests, nobles
  - Merchants, traders
  - Artisans, shop-keepers
  - Laborers, farmers
  - Slaves
- Only boys in school
- Strict laws
- Belief in many gods
- Belief in life after death

KEY ACHIEVEMENTS
- System of writing
- Crop irrigation systems
- Organized schools
- Advancement in mathematics
- Advancement in astronomy
- First calendar
- Organized religion
- Organized government
- Code of Hammurabi

EGYPT

KEY EVENTS

5000 B.C.	Cattle herders in Sahara
	Farming begins in Egypt
3300 B.C.	Hieroglyphic writing is developed
3118 B.C.	King Menes unites Egypt; becomes first pharaoh
2686-2181 B.C.	Old Kingdom - Dynasties III-VI, pyramids built
2667-2648 B.C.	Building of Step Pyramid
2133-1633 B.C.	Middle Kingdom - Dynasties XI-XIII
1567-1085 B.C.	New Kingdom
1503-1482 B.C.	Reign of Hatshepsut
1379-1362 B.C.	Reign of Akhenaton and Nefertiti
1361 B.C.	Tutankhamen rules
1286 B.C.	Moses leads Hebrews back to Palestine
1085 B.C.	Decline of Egyptian power

KEY PEOPLE
- Menes (1st ruler)
- Tutankhamen
- Queen Hatshepsut
- Thutmose III
- Rameses II
- Nefertiti
- Akhenaton
- Imhotep

KEY ACHIEVEMENTS
- Invented embalming
- Architectural and engineering feats:
  - Temples
  - Pyramids
  - Sphinx
  - Palaces
- Hieroglyphics
- Papyrus paper
- Educated scribes
- Medical knowledge
- Daily calendar
- First to use stone
- Columns
- Extensive trade
- Empire expansion

LIFE-STYLE
- Farm/trade culture
- Worship many gods (Amon-Re, king of gods)
- Worship cats, crocodiles
- Belief in afterlife
- Class system:
  - Pharaoh
  - Priests/nobles
  - Scribes
  - Artisans
  - Peasants/slaves

GODS
- Re
- Hathor
- Anabis
- Osiris
- Isis

KEY PLACES
- Nile River
- Egypt
- Giza

KEY TERMS
- Dynasty
- Pharaoh
- Papyrus
- Pyramids
- Empire Age
- Mummy
- Old Kingdom
- Middle Kingdom
- New Kingdom
- Obelisk

THE RISE OF CIVILIZATION (PREHISTORY—450 B.C.) *(cont.)*

ASIA MINOR, EASTERN MEDITERRANEAN, PERSIA

KEY EVENTS

2371-2230 B.C.	Establishment of Kingdom of Akkad
2000 B.C.	Hittites set up states in Anatolia
	Rise of Babylon
1814-1754 B.C.	First Assyrian Empire
1792-1750 B.C.	Reign of Hammurabi
1650-1450 B.C.	Hittite Old Kingdom
1595 B.C.	Hittites burn Babylon
1450-1200 B.C.	Hittite Empire (New Kingdom)
1375-1047 B.C.	Middle Assyrian Empire
1200 B.C.	Moses leads Hebrews to Canaan
1200-1000 B.C.	Phoenicians rise to power
1020 B.C.	Saul becomes King of Israel
1010-926 B.C.	United Jewish Kingdom of Israel
960 B.C.	Solomon rules Israel
911-609 B.C.	New Assyrian Empire
835 B.C.	Rise of Kingdom of Medes
680-652 B.C.	Kingdom of Lydia
627-539 B.C.	Neo-Babylonian Empire
586-538 B.C.	King Nebuchadnezzar II of Babylonia destroys Jerusalem
525 B.C.	Persians conquer Egypt

KEY PEOPLE
Hittites
Israelites (Hebrews)
Abraham
Moses
King David
Solomon
King Nebuchadnezzar
Saul
Cyrus
Darius

KEY PLACES
Asia Minor
Syria
Lebanon
Phoenicia
Canaan
Israel
Jerusalem
Persepolis

LIFE-STYLE
Sailors, shipbuilders
Merchants
Belief in one god

KEY ACHIEVEMENTS
Money economy
Ironworking
Royal purple dye
Clear glass
"Carriers of civilization"
First alphabet
Ten Commandments
Hebrew law

KEY TERMS
Iron Age
Monotheism
Judaism
Yahweh
Exodus
Torah
Prophets
Hebrews
Ten
  Commandments
Old Testament

ANCIENT INDIA AND CHINA

KEY EVENTS

5000 B.C.	Agriculture begins in China
2500-1500 B.C.	Indus Valley Civilization
1800-1500 B.C.	Hsia Dynasty rules China
1500 B.C.	Indus Valley Civilization collapses
1500-1028 B.C.	Shang Dynasty
1500-600 B.C.	Vedic Period in India
1028 B.C.	Chou Dynasty overthrows Shang Dynasty
660 B.C.	Emperor Jimmu founds Japan
600 B.C.	Introduction of Taoism
560-483 B.C.	Life of Gautama Siddhartha (Buddha)
551-479 B.C.	Life of Kung Fu-tze (Confucius)

KEY PEOPLE
- Aryans
- Confucius
- Li Po
- Yu
- Shang Dynasty
- Zhou Dynasty

KEY PLACES
- Indus Valley
- Mohenjo-Daro
- Harappa
- Chung Kwo
- Yellow River
- Himalayas
- Yangtze River

KEY TERMS
- Rajah
- Hinduism
- Reincarnation
- Dharma
- Karma
- Feudalism
- Bureaucrat
- Mandate of Heaven
- Dynasty
- Mandarin
- Filial piety

LIFE-STYLE
- Belief in many gods
- Deep respect for nature
- Caste system:
  - Warrior-nobles
  - Priests
  - Common people
  - Laboring class
- Extended family
- Obedience to elders
- Respect of ancient customs

KEY ACHIEVEMENTS
- Sewer systems
- Cotton cloth
- Measurement system
- Silk cloth
- System of feudalism
- Trained bureaucrats
- Confucian virtues:
  - Integrity
  - Generosity
  - Loyalty

CLASSICAL CIVILIZATION
(1700 B.C.–A.D. 950)

GREECE (1700 B.C - 30 B.C)

KEY EVENTS

1900-1200 B.C.	Mycenae Civilization
1250 B.C.	Trojan Wars
1050-750 B.C.	Dark Ages in Greece
800 B.C.	Homer composes *Iliad* and *Odyssey*
776 B.C.	First Olympic Games in Greece
750 B.C.	Beginning of Greek city-states
683 B.C.	Hereditary kings replaced by archons (chief magistrates) chosen yearly
600-500 B.C.	Archaic Period in Greek art
509-507 B.C.	Democratic form of government
500-338 B.C.	Classical Period in Greek art
490 & 480-479 B.C.	Persian Wars
431-404 B.C.	Peloponnesian Wars
336-323 B.C.	Empire of Alexander the Great
323-30 B.C.	Hellenistic Age

KEY ACHIEVEMENTS

Self-government (democracy)
Art
Sculpture
Architecture
Colonization
Olympics
Epics of Homer
Jury system
Citizenship
Literature
Drama
Philosophy
Natural scientific laws
Mathematics
Medicine
Libraries
Geometry

LIFE-STYLE

Belief in many gods
Celebrated religious festivals
Revered honor and courage
Trained for war
Encouraged talent
Men highly educated
Women considered inferior
Lived inside city walls
Farmed outside city walls

ANCIENT GODS

Aphrodite, goddess of love
Apollo, god of light, medicine, poetry
Ares, god of war
Artemis, goddess of hunting
Athena, goddess of crafts, war, wisdom
Cronus, Greek ruler of Titans
Demeter, goddess of agriculture
Eros, god of love
Hephaestus, blacksmith for the gods; god of fire and metalworking
Hera, protector of marriage and women
Hermes, messenger for the gods
Hestia, goddess of the hearth
Pluto (Hades), god of the underworld
Poseidon, god of the sea
Zeus, ruler of the gods

KEY PEOPLE
- Phidias
- Aristophanes
- Praxiteles
- Aesop
- Democritus
- Pythagorus
- Herodotus
- Thucydides
- Aeschylus
- Sophocles
- Euripides
- Thale
- Homer
- Minoans
- Mycenaeans
- Dorians
- Solon
- Pisistratus
- Pericles
- Archimedes
- Ptolemy
- Euclid
- Eratosthenes
- Hippocrates
- Socrates
- Plato
- Aristotle
- Demosthenes
- Philip
- Alexander the Great

KEY PLACES
- Sparta
- Athens
- Attica
- Marathon
- Salamis
- Macedonia
- Asia Minor
- Aegean Sea
- Peloponnesus
- Crete
- Thebes
- Mycenae
- Thermopylae

KEY TERMS
- Hellenic Age
- Acropolis
- Colony
- Oracle
- Epics
- Assembly
- Democracy
- Tyrant
- Demagogues
- Agora
- Ephors
- Tragedy
- Comedy
- Philosopher
- Socratic method
- Persian Wars
- Parthenon

ROME (700 B.C. - A.D. 180)

KEY EVENTS

753 B.C.	Founding of Rome
510-109 B.C.	Monarchy replaced by Republic
264-241 B.C.	First Punic War
218-201 B.C.	Second Punic War
	Hannibal invades Italy
215-205 B.C.	First Macedonian War between Macedonia and Rome
149-146 B.C.	Third Punic War
	Rome defeats Carthage
91-89 B.C.	War between Rome and her allies ends with allies becoming Roman citizens
82-79 B.C.	Sulla is dictator of Rome
73-71 B.C.	Roman slave, Spartacus, leads an unsuccessful revolt
60 B.C.	Rome is ruled by the First Triumvirate: Julius Caesar, Pompey, and Crassus
58-51 B.C.	Gaul (France) conquered by Julius Caesar
49-45 B.C.	Civil war between Julius Caesar and Pompey
	Caesar becomes dictator
46 B.C.	Julius Caesar introduces Julian calendar
44 B.C.	Julius Caesar assassinated; civil war follows
31 B.C.	Octavian establishes his leadership of Rome in Battle of Actium
27 B.C.	Roman Republic ends; Octavian becomes Emperor Augustus
A.D. 43	Romans conquer Britain
A.D. 98-117	Height of Roman Empire under Emperor Trajan
A.D. 122-127	Hadrian's Wall built on Rome's northern frontier in Britain
A.D. 200	Germanic tribes attack frontiers of Roman Empire
A.D. 300	Huns invade Europe
A.D. 391	Christianity becomes Roman state religion
A.D. 395	Decline of the Roman Empire

KEY PLACES

Tiber River
Rome
Roman Empire
Alps
Mediterranean Sea
Sicily
Constantinople

KEY PEOPLE

Etruscans
Hannibal
Attila the Hun
Gnaeus Pompey
Marcus Licinius Crassus
Julius Caesar
Tiberius
Marcus Brutus
Gais Cassius
Lepidus
Octavian (Augustus)
Spartacus
Marcus Aurelius Antonius
Hadrian
Trajan
Caligula
Claudius
Nero
Virgil
Horace
Ptolemy
Galen
Cicero
Livy
Constantine

KEY TERMS

Republic
Patrician
Plebeian
Dictator
Senate
Triumvirate
Pax Romana
Circus Maximus
Colosseum
Aqueduct
Gladiator
Oratory
Law of succession
Visigoth

LIFE-STYLE

Upper class:
- Wealthy landowners
- Government officials
- Merchants
- Doctors
- Lawyers
- Scholars
- Writers
- Artists

Upper class possessions:
- Luxurious town houses
- Large country houses
- Swimming pools
- Fine silk clothes
- Jewelry

Lower class (poor):
- Farmers (majority)
- Slaves
- Dependent on government support
- Public homes
- Free food

Family life:
- Women had freedom
- Boys educated at school
- Girls educated at home

Entertainment:
- Chariot races
- Gladiators

Religion:
- Gods and goddesses
- Ancestor worship
- Christianity
- Judaism

GODS AND GODDESSES

- Apollo, god of light, medicine, and poetry
- Ceres, goddess of agriculture
- Cupid, god of love
- Diana, goddess of hunting
- Juno, protector of marriage and women
- Jupiter, ruler of the gods
- Mars, god of war
- Mercury, messenger for the gods
- Minerva, goddess of crafts, war, and wisdom
- Neptune, god of the sea
- Pluto, god of the underworld
- Saturn, god of agriculture
- Venus, goddess of love
- Vesta, goddess of the hearth
- Vulcan, blacksmith for the gods; god of fire, metalworking

KEY ACHIEVEMENTS

- Road building
- Sanitation
- Architecture
- Republic form of government
- Roman army
- Julian calendar
- Water systems
- Roman Empire expansion
- Trade flourished
- Expanded citizenship
- Cultural achievements
- Circus Maximus
- Engineering skills
- Literature
- Roman law and justice
- Spread of Christianity

INDIA AND JAPAN (565 B.C. - A.D. 589)

KEY EVENTS

327-325 B.C.	Alexander the Great invades India
321-185 B.C.	Maurya Dynasty founded in India
300 B.C. - A.D. 300	Bronze-making skills introduced to Japan by Chinese and Korean travelers
272-231 B.C.	Reign of King Asoka (Maurya Dynasty) unites northern and central India
200 B.C.	Three kingdoms established in India
	Greeks invade India
	Greek states established in the Punjab
150 B.C. - A.D. 50	Bronze Age culture in North Vietnam
A.D. 50	Bactrians invade northern India, establish Kushan Empire
A.D. 180	Tribal groups unite in India
A.D. 195-405	Parthians control northern India
A.D. 285	Writing introduced to Japan
A.D. 300	Yamato government established in Japan
A.D. 316	Empress Jingo of Japan invades Korea
A.D. 320-532	Chandragupta II founds Gupta Empire
A.D. 430-470	Huns invade India
	Gupta Empire declines

KEY PEOPLE
Siddhartha Gautama
   (Buddha)
King Magadha
Cyrus the Great
Darius I
Asoka
Kalidasa
Dravidians
Aryabhata
Chandragupta Maurya

KEY ACHIEVEMENTS
Gupta literature
Mathematics:
   decimal system
   concept of zero
   algebra
Large libraries

LIFE-STYLE
Caste system
Honored elders
Revered teachers
Respect for life
Religion:
   Hinduism
   Buddhism

KEY PLACES
India
Nepal
Tibet
Burma
China
Mongolia
Afghanistan
Korea
Japan
Southeast Asia
Ceylon
Malaya
Java
Ganges River
Himalayas
Indus River
Punjab

KEY TERMS
Buddhism
Four Noble Truths
Nirvana
Hinduism
Buddha
Ahimsa
Sanskrit
Mauryan Empire
Emperor
Gupta Empire
Caste
Untouchables
Rajas
Vedas
Reincarnation

CHINA (700 B.C. - A.D. 950)

KEY EVENTS

650 B.C.	Iron-making in China
600 B.C.	Taoism introduced
551-479 B.C.	Life of Confucius
221-206 B.C.	Ch'in Dynasty
214 B.C.	Great Wall of China is built
206 B.C. - A.D. 222	Han Dynasty rules China
140- 87 B.C.	China expands under Emperor Wu-Ti
A.D. 9	Wang Mang sets up Hsin Dynasty
A.D. 25-222	Han Dynasty is restored
A.D. 91	Chinese defeat the Huns in Mongolia

KEY PEOPLE
Mencius
Laozi (Lao-tzu)
Li Si
Gao Zu
Wu Ti

KEY PLACES
Yellow Sea
Yangtze (Ch'ang) River
Wei River Valley

KEY TERMS
Taoism
Great Wall
Legalism
Silk Road
Dynastic cycle
Age of Disunity
Tao Te Ching

KEY ACHIEVEMENTS
Great Wall
Roads
Canals
Silk cloth
Civil service exams
Calendar
Water clocks
Sun dials
Star maps
Astronomical principles
Magnetic compass
Medical discoveries
Paper
Porcelain china
Philosophy

AFRICA (1600 B.C. - A.D. 950)

KEY EVENTS

5000-2000 B.C.	Sahara Desert formed
1600 B.C. - A.D. 400	Kingdom of Kush
1525 B.C.	Egypt conquers Kush
1379-1362 B.C.	Reign of Akhenaton
814 B.C.	Carthage founded
715 B.C.	Kush conquers Egypt
700 B.C.	Domestication of cattle and sheep
671 B.C.	Assyrians invade Egypt
525-404 B. C.	Persia conquers Egypt
500 B.C. - A.D. 200	Rise of Nok culture
500 B.C. - A.D. 400	Nubian kings move capital to Meroc
332 B.C.	Alexander the Great conquers Egypt
323-30 B.C.	Ptolemaic Dynasty and rise of Alexandria as a cultural center
146 B.C.	Rome conquers Carthage
30 B.C.	Cleopatra defeated; Rome conquers Egypt
A.D. 70	Christianity spreads to Alexandria
A.D. 100	Rise of Aksum culture
	Camel caravans open desert trade routes

KEY PEOPLE
Nok people
Bantu people
Kushites
Cleopatra
Soninkes

KEY PLACES
Nile Valley
Congo River Basin
Sahara, Kalahari, and
Namib Deserts
Nigeria and Ghana
Great Rift Valley
Senegal River
Upper Niger River

KEY ACHIEVEMENTS
Iron-making
Jewelry
Furniture-making
Pottery design

LIFE-STYLE
Farmers
Herders
Skilled metalworkers
Many languages
Traders
Ironworkers
Very rich kings

KEY TERMS
Savannas
Desert
Ivory
Ebony
Islam
Silent barter
Ships of the desert
Sub-Saharan
Oasis

THE AMERICAS (2000 B.C. - A.D. 1000)

KEY EVENTS

2000-1000 B.C.	Mayan culture begins
1500 B.C.	North American people begin farming
1500 B.C. - A.D. 200	Olmec culture in Mexico
900-200 B.C.	Chavin culture of Peru flourishes
700 B.C.	Founding of Monte Alban
600-200 B.C.	Adena people of North America construct earthen buildings and burial mounds
300 B.C.	Decline of Olmec culture; rise of Zapotec culture
200 B.C. - A.D. 700	Rise of Teotihuacan culture in Mexico
A.D. 250-600	Peak of Mayan Civilization
A.D. 400	Rise of Inca culture
A.D. 500	North America: Mississippi mound builders appear
A.D. 500-900	Golden age of the Zapotec culture in Mexico
A.D. 650-900	Huastecan culture in Mexico
A.D. 700-1000	North America: Hohokam farming communities in Arizona Anasazi farmers emerge in North America, build pueblos
A.D. 750	Mayan Civilization begins decline
A.D. 986	Eric the Red colonizes Greenland
A.D. 1000	Leif Ericson travels down the American coast

KEY PEOPLE
- Pachacuti
- Mayas
- Aztecs
- Incas
- Olmecs

KEY PLACES
- Yucatan
- Lake Texcoco
- Tenochtitlan
- Cuzco
- Teotihuacan

KEY TERMS
- Maize
- Quipu
- Llama
- Alpaca

LIFE-STYLE
- Cities were centers of religion
- Upper class:
  - Priests
  - Nobles
  - Warriors
- Peasants:
  - Soldiers
  - Farmers
- Women could not hold public office or enter temples

KEY ACHIEVEMENTS
- Science/astronomy
- Government
- Arts
- Pyramids
- Accurate calendar
- Advanced mathematical skills
- Concept of zero
- Maya city-states

THE MEDIEVAL WORLD
(300–1500)

BYZANTINE AND RUSSIAN CIVILIZATIONS (300 - 1500)
(The Eastern Roman Empire)

KEY EVENTS

330	Constantinople built
527-565	Justinian rules Byzantine Empire, reuniting the Roman Empire
603-628	Byzantine Empire defeats Persia
793-794	Vikings begin raiding Europe
890-1015	Vladimir, Grand Prince of Kiev, rules Russia
988	Christianity becomes official religion in Russia
1054	Christian church divides
1096-1099	First Crusade
1147-1149	Second Crusade
1189-1192	Third Crusade
1204	Crusaders capture Constantinople
1480	Ivan III ends Mongol rule of Russia

KEY PEOPLE
Justinian
Theodora
Vladimir
Slavs
Vikings
Mongols
OttomanTurks
Genghis Khan
Ivan the Great

KEY TERMS
Justinian's Code
Roman Catholic Church
Eastern Orthodox Church
Hagia Sophia
Golden Horde
Icon
Crusades
Czar

KEY PLACES
Constantinople
Byzantine Empire
Kiev
Novgorod
Moscow

KEY ACHIEVEMENTS
Root of modern day system of laws
Center of wealth and culture
Trade center
Architectural innovations

THE MEDIEVAL WORLD (300-1500) *(cont.)*

THE WORLD OF ISLAM (470 - 1258)

KEY EVENTS

570	Mohammed born
618-619	Persians conquer Egypt
622	Mohammed leads Hegira
632	Mohammed dies
661	Islam splits
661-750	Umayyads rule Muslim Empire
700's	Flourishing trade routes in Sahara Desert
750-1258	Abbasids rule Muslim Empire
1258	Mongols destroy Baghdad

KEY PEOPLE
Mohammed
Abu Bakr
Umayyads Dynasty
Abbasids Dynasty
Mongols
Avicenna
Averroes
Harun al-Rashid
Omar Khayyam
Rhazes

KEY ACHIEVEMENTS
Universities developed
Philosophy
Arabic number system
Geometry
Trigonometry
Persian rugs
Water pipes
Paved, lighted streets
Efficient agriculture
Rotation of crops
Canon of medicine
Literature:
> *1001 Arabian Nights*
> *Sinbad the Sailor*
> *Aladdin*

LIFE-STYLE
Nomadic
Prized learning
Valued tribal loyalty
Personal honor
Worshipped tribal gods before Mohammed
Practiced religious tolerance
Slaves' lives improved
More than one wife allowed
Women lived restricted lives

KEY PLACES
Arabia
Mecca
Medina
Baghdad
Holy Land
Cordov
Cairo
Damascus
Persian Gulf

KEY TERMS
Bedouin
Islam
Muslim
Koran
Five Pillars of Islam
Hegira
Jihad
Sunni
Shiite
Caliph
Sultans
Mosque
Minaret

MEDIEVAL EUROPE (730 - 1460)

KEY EVENTS		KEY TERMS
732	Muslims defeated at Battle of Tours	Middle Ages
800	Charlemagne crowned emperor	Feudalism
871	Alfred the Great begins rule of England	Manorial system
1002	Vikings sail to North America	Middle class
1066	William the Conqueror invades England	Battle of Hastings
1088	University of Bologna established	Common law
1096	First Crusade begins	Magna Carta
1122	Concordat of Worms	Parliament
1200	Coins are used for trade	Absolute monarchy
1215	Magna Carta signed by King John	Inquisition
1265	Dante born	Romanesque
1300	Feudalism declines	Gothic
1337-1453	Hundred Years' War	Black Death
1340	Chaucer born	Nation-state
1347	Plague spreads throughout Europe	Guild
1455	Wars of the Roses	Merchant
		Apprentice

KEY PEOPLE   LIFE-STYLE

KEY TERMS (cont.): Journeyman, Master, Crusader, Medieval, Papacy, Sacrament, Clergy, Fief, Vassal, Knight, Chivalry, Manor

KEY PEOPLE
- Pope Gregory I
- Venerable Bede
- Saint Benedict
- Saint Patrick
- Clovis
- Charlemagne
- Eleanor of Aquitaine
- Alfred the Great
- William the Conqueror
- King John
- Philip Augustus
- Pope Gregory II
- Henry IV
- Pope Innocent III
- Saint Dominic
- Saint Francis of Assisi
- Thomas Aquinas
- Roger Bacon
- Dante
- Geoffrey Chaucer
- Joan of Arc
- Henry VII
- Magyars
- Normans
- Tudors

LIFE-STYLE
- Level of learning dropped
- Lost Latin, Greek languages
- Only clergy learned to write
- Marriage considered sacred
- Women have prestige
- Serfs worked three days a week for manor lord
- Serfs' life difficult
- Rise of middle class
- Peasant rebellions

KEY ACHIEVEMENTS
- Cities grew
- Guilds organized
- Castles built
- Banking
- Revival of learning
- Universities
- Drama
- Vernacular languages
- Religious art
- Romanesque architecture
- Gothic architecture
- Development of longbow

23

RENAISSANCE AND REFORMATION
(1350–1600)

KEY EVENTS

1350	Renaissance begins in Italy
1337-1453	Hundred Years' War between France and England
1429	Joan of Arc leads French army against England
1450	Johann Gutenberg invents the printing press
1469	Ferdinand and Isabella marry, uniting Spain
1492	Christopher Columbus discovers the Americas
1494	France invades Italy
1505	Leonardo da Vinci paints the Mona Lisa
1508	Michelangelo paints the Sistine Chapel
1517	Reformation begins when Martin Luther breaks away from the Roman Catholic Church
1534	Henry VIII establishes Church of England
1543	Nicholas Copernicus publishes scientific ideas
1558	Elizabeth I crowned Queen of England
1564	Shakespeare is born
1588	England defeats Spanish Armada
1605	Cervantes' *Don Quixote* is published
1609	Galileo improves the telescope
1648	Netherlands wins independence from Spain
1687	Isaac Newton publishes his ideas about gravity

KEY PEOPLE
Medici family
Giotto
Leonardo da Vinci
Michelangelo Buonarroti
Lorenzo the Magnificent
Moors
Johann Gutenberg
Martin Luther
Philip II
Henry VIII
Elizabeth Tudor
William Shakespeare
Joan of Arc
Nicholas Copernicus
Isaac Newton
Galileo
Desiderius Erasmus
Sir Thomas More
Miguel de Cervantes
Rembrandt

LIFE-STYLE
Rich "merchant princes"
Education important
Love of ancient Greek and Roman culture
Appreciated nature

KEY ACHIEVEMENTS
Constitutions
Elected governments
Great art
Science
Inventions
Appearance of cannons and crude handguns
Printing press
Movable type
Bookmaking
Famous plays
Scientific method

KEY PLACES
Florence, Italy
Arno River
Wittenberg

KEY TERMS
Patrons
Perspective
Mercenaries
Alliances
Heresy
Reformation
Monarchs
Heir
Armada
Protestant
Elizabethan Age
Heliocentric

EUROPEAN EXPLORATION & COLONIZATION
(1450–1763)

KEY MOTIVES BEHIND EXPLORATION
- Desire for wealth and power
- Religious aims
- Renaissance spirit
- Technological progress:
  - Sailing ships
  - More accurate maps
  - Weaponry for protection
  - Navigational instruments

KEY MOTIVES BEHIND COLONIZATION
- Escape religious conflicts
- Economic growth

KEY EXPLORATIONS AND COLONIES

1394-1460	Portugal sets up trading posts and sugar plantations in West Africa
1488	Portuguese explorer Batholomeu Dias sails around tip of Africa (Cape of Good Hope)
1492	Christopher Columbus, searching for a westward route to India, lands in the West Indies and opens up the Americas for colonization
1497	King of Portugal sends Vasco da Gama to India to set up sea trade routes
	King Henry VII sends John Cabot to America; he finds Newfoundland
1499	Amerigo Vespucci makes several voyages to the Americas for both Spain and Portugal
1500	Pedro Cabral claims Brazil for Portugal; settlements soon follow
1508-1513	Ponce de Leon establishes a colony in Puerto Rico and explores Florida
1513	Vasco de Balboa establishes a settlement in Panama and crosses the Isthmus of Panama, making him the first European to see the Pacific Ocean
1519	Ferdinand Magellan, a Portuguese navigator, sets sail to circumnavigate the globe with 5 ships and 265 men. Many sailors die, including Magellan; however, in 1522 one ship with 18 crew members completes the voyage
	Hernando Cortes explores Mexico, eventually taking control of it from the Aztecs
1532	Francisco Pizarro arrives in South America and, after killing hundreds of Incas, eventually is assassinated by one of his own men; a colony is set up in Peru
1535	Jacques Cartier of France claims eastern Canada
1540	Francisco de Coronado travels north from Mexico into Colorado
1541	Hernando de Soto explores Florida, as far north as the Carolinas, and as far west as the Mississippi River
1542	Spanish missionary, Bartolome de las Casas, appeals to the king of Spain for laws protecting Indians in Mexico
Late 1500s	Many Catholic friars come to the Americas to convert the Indians

1597	Henry Hudson, an English explorer, makes four voyages in search of the Northwest Passage; in 1609, sailing for Dutch merchants, he finds the Hudson River and establishes the colony of New Netherlands (New York City)
1600s–1700s	English settlers establish colonies in Canada, America, and on the Caribbean islands
1602	The Netherlands establishes the Dutch East India Company which takes over nearly all the Portuguese ports in Asia, including Japan
1608	Samuel de Champlain establishes Quebec
1621	Dutch East India Company controls most of the shipping and slave trade to the Americas and the Caribbean
1672	French fur traders Jacques Marquette and Louis Joliet explore the Great Lakes and the Wisconsin and Mississippi Rivers
1682	Sieur de La Salle, a French nobleman, claims the Mississippi Valley for France and names it Louisiana in honor of King Louis XIV

KEY PLACES	KEY PEOPLE	KEY TERMS
West Africa	Prince Henry the Navigator	Line of Demarcation
Cape of Good Hope	Bartholomeu Dias	Circumnavigate
West Indies	Vasco da Gama	Conquistadors
Caribbean	Christopher Columbus	Viceroy
Cuba	Amerigo Vespucci	Peon
Haiti	Ponce de Leon	Encomiendas
Hispanola	Vasco de Balboa	Northwest Passage
Panama	Ferdinand Magellan	Privateers
Florida	Montezuma	Puritans
Mexico	Atahualpa	Quakers
Tenochtitlan	Hernando Cortes	
Peru	Malinche	
Newfoundland	Cuauhtemoc	
Brazil	Francisco Pizarro	
Quebec	Hernando de Soto	
Hudson River	Francisco de Coronado	
Canada	Bartolome de las Casas	
Louisiana	Sieur de La Salle	
Mississippi River	Pedro Cabral	
	John Cabot	
	Henry Hudson	
	Jacques Cartier	
	Samuel de Champlain	
	Louis Joliet	
	Jacques Marquette	

SEEKING REFORM AND INDEPENDENCE (1500–1900)

KEY EVENTS

1517	Luther issues his 95 theses
1519	Zwingli begins preaching reform in Zurich
1523	Sweden gains independence from Denmark
1536	Inca rebellion in Peru
1541	The Reformation begins in Scotland
	Indian revolt in Mexico
1543	Copernicus' theories launch Scientific Revolution
1572	Beginning of the Dutch Revolt
1633	Galileo is brought before Inquisition
1651	Hobbes's *Leviathan* is published
1665	Portugal secures independence from Spain
1687	Newton's *Principia* is published
1707	England and Scotland unite; renamed Great Britain
1708	Revolution in Ethiopia
1748	Montesquieu's *Spirit of the Law* is published
1750	Enlightenment reaches its height
1769	Watt develops practical steam engine
1770	Sturm und Drang movement develops in Germany
1770s	Start of great age of European orchestral music
1774	Louis XVI becomes king of France
1775–1783	American War of Independence
1776	American Declaration of Independence
1780	Tupac Amaru leads rebellion in Peru
1783	Treaty of Paris recognizes America's independence
1787	Adoption of United States Constitution
1789	French Revolution begins
1793	Whitney invents cotton gin
	Louis XVI and Marie Antoinette are executed
1793–1794	Reign of Terror in France
1799	Napoleon overthrows Directory
1804	Napoleon is crowned emperor of France
	Haiti gains independence
1810	Argentina declares independence from Spain
1811	Paraguay and Venezuela declare independence
1813	Colombia declares independence
1814	Congress of Vienna begins
	Uruguay declares independence
1815	Italian nationalist groups form
	Battle of Waterloo

KEY PEOPLE

- Andreas Vesalius
- Nicholas Copernicus
- Isaac Newton
- Johannes Kepler
- Francis Bacon
- Rene Descartes
- Thomas Hobbes
- John Locke
- Voltaire
- Baron de Montesquieu
- Jean Jacques Rousseau
- Johann Sebastian Bach
- Wolfgang Amadeus Mozart
- Ludwig van Beethoven
- George Washington
- Thomas Jefferson
- Benjamin Franklin
- Louis XVI
- Marie Antoinette
- Maximillian Robespierre
- Pierre Toussaint
- Miguel Hidalgo
- Porfirio Diaz
- Louis Philippe
- John Keats
- Charlotte Bronte
- Eugene Delacroix
- Lord Byron
- Giuseppe Verde
- Napoleon Bonaparte
- Simon Bolivar
- Benito Juarez
- Klemens von Metternich
- William Wordsworth
- Mary Shelley
- Emily Bronte
- Sir Walter Scott
- Richard Wagner
- Louis Napoleon

SEEKING REFORM AND INDEPENDENCE (1500–1900) *(cont.)*

KEY EVENTS *(continued)*

1816	Chile declares independence
1820	Revolts in Spain and Italy
1823	Monroe Doctrine
1824	Bolivar completes the liberation of South America
1829-	
1884	British Parliament makes democratic reforms
1829	Greece wins independence
1830	Revolts in France, Belgium, and Poland
	Stevenson develops locomotive
1839	El Salvador, Honduras, Nicaragua, Guatemala, and Costa Rica become independent
1846-	
1848	Mexican-American War
1847	Liberia becomes independent
1848	Revolutions sweep Europe (France, Austria, Italy, Germany, Hungary)
	Marx and Engels publish *Communist Manifesto*
1853-	
1856	Crimean War
1858	War of the Reform
1860	Impressionist movement begins
1861-	
1865	American Civil War
1866	Juarez regains power from Maximilian
	Tolstoy's *War and Peace* is published
1874	Iceland becomes independent
1876	Korea wins independence from China
1876-	
1911	Diaz rules Mexico
1877-	
1878	Romania, Montenegro, and Serbia gain independence from Turkey
1896	Herzl calls for Jewish homeland

KEY ACHIEVEMENTS

Scientific method
Scientific discoveries
Study of living things
Microscopes
Philosophy
Political reforms
Classical style in arts
U. S. Constitution
Many inventions

KEY PLACES

Yorktown
Trafalgar
Elba
St. Helena

KEY TERMS

Scientific Revolution
Enlightenment
Natural rights
American Revolution
Constitution
Checks and balances
Old Regime
French Revolution
Declaration of
 the Rights of Man
Jacobin
Reign of Terror
Coup d'etat
Napoleonic Wars
Quadruple Alliance
Neocolonialism
Liberalism
Sturm und Drang
Scientific method
Social contract
Separation of powers
Declaration of
 Independence
Federal system
Bill of Rights
Bourgeoisie
Radical
Suffrage
Girondist
Nationalism
Napoleonic Code
Continental System
Monroe Doctrine
Conservatism
Socialism
Industrial Revolution

WARS AND UNREST
(1880–1945)

KEY EVENTS

1882	Germany allies with Austria-Hungary and Italy (Triple Alliance)
1894	Nicholas II becomes Czar of Russia
1905	Workers in St. Petersburg revolt
1907	Alliance among France, Britain, and Russia (Triple Entente)
1914	World War I begins with assassination of Archduke Ferdinand of Austria-Hungary
1915	Italy joins the Allies
	Lusitania sinks
1916	British use tanks
1917	China and Siam join the Allies in World War I
	American ships are sunk by German submarines; United States declares war on Germany
	Lenin comes to power in Bolshevik Revolution
1918	Armistice ends fighting in World War I
1919	Treaty of Versailles signed
	League of Nations formed
1922	Mussolini comes to power in Italy
	USSR is formed
1923	Republic of Turkey is created
1926	Hirohito becomes emperor of Japan
1928	Kellogg-Briand Pact
1929	Great Depression begins in United States
	Stalin comes to power in Soviet Union
1931	Japan invades Manchuria
1933	Hitler forms Third Reich in Germany
	New Deal begins in the United States
1934-1935	Long March in China
1935-1939	Great Purge in Soviet Union
1936	Alliance between Germany and Italy
1936-1939	Spanish Civil War
1939	World War II begins
1940	Hitler invades France; Battle of Britain begins
1941	Japanese attack Pearl Harbor; U.S. enters war
1942	Battle of Midway
1944	Allied forces land in Normandy
1945	End of World War II; Germany and Japan surrender

KEY TERMS

World War I
Triple Alliance
Triple Entente
Kaiser
Allies
U-boat
Fourteen Points
League of Nations
Treaty of Versailles
Central Powers
Bolshevik
March Revolution
Kremlin
Ideology
Totalitarianism
Socialism
Facism
Communism
Isolationism
Militarism
Nazi Party
Great Depression
Spanish Civil War
New Deal
Commonwealth of Nations
Axis Powers
Nazi-Soviet Pact
World War II
Concentration camp
Holocaust
D-Day
United Nations

WARS AND UNREST (1880–1945) *(cont.)*

KEY PEOPLE
Francis Ferdinand
Woodrow Wilson
Nicholas II
Vladimir Lenin
Rasputin
Alexander Kerensky
Leon Trotsky
Joseph Stalin
Benito Mussolini
Adolf Hitler
Heinrich Himmler
Francisco Franco
Franklin Delano Roosevelt
Sun Yat-sen
Chiang Kai-shek
Mao Zedong
Reza Shah Pahlavi
Ibn Saud
Haile Selassie
Neville Chamberlain
Winston Churchill
Dwight D. Eisenhower
Charles de Gaulle
Harry Truman
Douglas MacArthur

KEY PLACES
Austria-Hungary
Serbia
St. Petersburg
Palestine
Sudetenland
Auschwitz
Pearl Harbor
Normandy
Iwo Jima
Hiroshima
Nagasaki
Prussia
Berlin

KEY ACHIEVEMENTS
Political rights for women
Automobiles
Airplanes
Vacuum cleaners
Telephones
Washing machines
Radios
Movies
Surrealism painting
Walt Disney's animated film *Fantasia*

THE CONTEMPORARY WORLD
(1945–2000)

KEY EVENTS

1945	United Nations established
1947	Marshall Plan
	India and Pakistan gain independence
1948	State of Israel is established
	First Arab-Israeli War
1948-	
1952	Europe receives aid through Marshall Plan
1949	Western powers form NATO
	Communists come to power in China
1951	Mau Mau movement begins in Kenya
1952	Puerto Rico becomes a commonwealth
	End of U.S. occupation of Japan
1953	End of the Korean War
1956	Suez Canal Crisis
1957	Soviet Union launches *Sputnik*
	Common Market formed
	Vietnam War begins
	Ghana gains independence
1959	Castro takes power in Cuba
1960	OPEC formed
1962	Cuban Missile Crisis
1963-	
1975	American involvement in Vietnam
1965	Voting Rights Act in U.S.
1966	Chinese cultural revolution
1967	Israel wins Six-Day War
	First successful human heart transplant
1967-	
1970	Nigerian Civil War
1968	Soviet Union invades Czechoslovakia
1969	U.S. astronauts land on the moon
1973	October War between Israel and Arab countries
1975	Lebanese Civil War
	North and South Vietnam united
1976	Soweto uprisings in South Africa
1977	Panama Canal Treaty
1978	Camp David Accords
1979	Iran takes U.S. hostages
	U.S. and China establish diplomatic relations
	Margaret Thatcher becomes Britain's prime minister
	Sandinistas take power in Nicaragua

KEY PEOPLE

Nikita Kruschev
Martin Luther King, Jr.
John F. Kennedy
Charles de Gaulle
Francois Mitterrand
Margaret Thatcher
Mikhail Gorbachev
Andrei Sakharov
Lech Walesa
Mao Zedong
Deng Xiaoping
Richard Nixon
Mohandas K. Gandhi
Indira Gandhi
Corazon Aquino
Ho Chi Minh
Lyndon B. Johnson
Gamal Abdel Nasser
Anwar el-Sadat
Jimmy Carter
Menachem Begin
Mohammed Reza Pahlavi
Ayatollah Khomeini
Saddam Hussein
Nelson Mandela
Desmond Tutu
F. W. de Klerk
Juan Peron
Salvador Allende
Fidel Castro
Ronald Reagan
George Bush
Bill Clinton
Boris Yeltsin

KEY EVENTS *(continued)*

1980	Solidarity formed in Poland
	Iran-Iraq War
1981	First space shuttle launched in U.S.
1985	Guatemala and Brazil elect civilian governments
	Gorbachev takes power in Soviet Union
1986	Space shuttle *Challenger* explodes
1987	Palestinians protest in occupied territories—Intifada
1988	Soviets withdraw from Afghanistan
1989	Collapse of Soviet domination of Eastern Europe
	Civilian government restored in Chile
	Pro-democracy demonstrations in China
1990	Germany is unified
	Nelson Mandela released from prison
1990-1991	U.S. forces in Middle East
1991	Persian Gulf War
	Soviet Union disbanded in December
1991-1992	Civil war in former Yugoslavia: Bosnia and Herzegovina, Croatia, Macedonia, and Slovenia become separate countries
1993	End of apartheid government in South Africa
1994	U.S. and U.N. forces help Aristide return to power in Haiti
	Palestinian authorities granted limited self-rule in Gaza and the West Bank
1995	Fiftieth anniversary of the United Nations

KEY ACHIEVEMENTS

Space shuttle
Satellite communications
Genetic engineering
Medical advances
Computer technology
Robotics
Environmental awareness
New energy sources
Global economy

KEY TERMS

Cold War
Marshall Plan
NATO
Warsaw Pact
Cuban Missile Crisis
Terrorism
Detente
Dissident
Perestroika
Glasnost
Cultural Revolution
Civil disobedience
Korean War
Vietnam War
PLO
OPEC
Iran-Iraq War
Gulf War
Apartheid
Civil rights
Third World

KEY PLACES

Berlin	South Africa
Gdansk	Nambia
Suez Canal	Puerto Rico
Sinai Peninsula	Bay of Pigs
West Bank	Nicaragua
Persian Gulf	Panama
Saudi Arabia	

EXPLORERS
OF THE WORLD

DATES	EXPLORER	NATIONALITY
331-326 B.C.	Alexander the Great	Macedonian
300 B.C.	Pytheas	Greek
128-126 B.C.	Zhang Qian	Chinese
982	Eric the Red	Norwegian
1000	Leif Ericson	Norwegian
1253-1255	William of Rubruck	Flemish
1271-1295	Marco Polo	Italian
1314-1330	Odoric of Pordenone	Italian
1325-1354	Ibn Batuta	Arabian
1487-1488	Bartolomeu Dias	Portuguese
1492-1504	Christopher Columbus	Italian
1497-1498	John Cabot	Italian
1498	Vasco da Gama	Portuguese
1499-1504	Amerigo Vespucci	Italian
1500-1501	Pedro Alvares Cabral	Portuguese
1513	Juan Ponce de Leon	Spanish
1513	Vasco Nunez de Balboa	Spanish
1519-1521	Ferdinand Magellan	Portuguese
1519-1521	Hernando Cortes	Spanish
1524	Giovanni da Verrazano	Italian
1526-1530	Sebastian Cabot	Italian
1528-1536	Alvar Nunez Cabeza de Vaca	Spanish
1531-1535	Francisco Pizarro	Spanish
1535	Jacques Cartier	French
1539-1542	Hernando de Soto	Spanish
1540-1542	Francisco de Coronado	Spanish
1541	Francisco de Orellana	Spanish
1576-1578	Sir Martin Frobisher	English
1577-1580	Sir Francis Drake	English
1598-1605	Juan de Onate	Spanish
1603-1616	Samuel de Champlain	French
1606	Willem Jansz	Dutch
1609-1611	Henry Hudson	English

1616	William Baffin	English
1642	Abel Janszoon Tasman	Dutch
1659-1661	Pierre Esprit Radisson	French
1673	Jacques Marquette	French
1673	Louis Jolliet	French-Canadian
1678-1687	Sieur Duluth	French
1679-1682	Henri de Tonti	French
1679-1682	Sieur de La Salle	French
1680	Louis Hennepin	Belgian
1691-1701	William Dampier	English
1727-1729	Vitus Bering	Danish
1731-1743	Sieur de La Verendrye	French-Canadian
1766-1769	Louis Antoine de Bougainville	French
1768-1779	James Cook	English
1770	James Bruce	Scottish
1789-1793	Sir Alexander Mackenzie	Canadian
1789-1812	David Thompson	Canadian
1795-1806	Mungo Park	Scottish
1804-1806	Meriwether Lewis	American
1804-1806	William Clark	American
1805-1807	Zebulon Pike	American
1819-1821	Fabian von Bellingshausen	Russian
1819-1845	Sir John Franklin	English
1820	Edward Bransfield	English
1822-1826	Alexander Gordon Laing	Scottish
1822-1827	Hugh Clapperton	Scottish
1824-1825	James Bridger	American
1824-1829	Jedediah Strong Smith	American
1826-1828	Rene Caillie	French
1827	Sir William E. Parry	English
1829-1830	Charles Sturt	English
1831-1843	Sir James Clark Ross	British
1840-1841	Edward John Eyre	English
1840	Charles Wilkes	American
1842-1846	John Charles Fremont	American
1849-1873	David Livingstone	Scottish
1850-1854	Sir Robert McClure	British

1853-1858	Sir Richard Burton	English
1858-1862	John McDouall Stuart	Scottish
1858	John Hanning Speke	English
1860-1861	Robert O'Hara Burke	Irish
1860-1861	William John Wills	English
1873	Peter Egerton Warburton	English
1874-1889	Sir Henry Stanley	Welsh
1878-1879	Nils A. E. Nordenskjold	Swedish
1878-1892	Emin Pasha	German
1888-1895	Fridtjof Nansen	Norwegian
1897-1941	Robert A. Bartlett	Canadian-American
1906-1918	Vilhjalmur Stefansson	American
1907-1916	Sir Ernest H. Shackleton	Irish
1909	Matthew A. Henson	American
1909	Robert Edwin Peary	American
1911-1926	Roald Amundsen	Norwegian
1912	Robert Falcon Scott	British
1926-1929	Richard Evelyn Byrd	American
1926	Umberto Nobile	Italian
1934	William Beebe	American
1951-1970s	Jacques-Yves Cousteau	French
1957-1958	Sir Edmund Hillary	New Zealander
1957-1958	Sir Vivian Fuchs	English
1958	William R. Anderson	American
1960	Don Walsh	American
1960	Jacques Piccard	Swiss
1961	Yuri A. Gagarin	Soviet
1963	Valentina V. Tereshkova	Soviet
1965	Alexei A. Leonov	Soviet
1968	Frank Borman	American
1968	James A. Lovell, Jr.	American
1968	William A. Anders	American
1969	Edwin E. Aldrin, Jr.	American
1969	Neil A. Armstrong	American
1981	John W. Young	American
1981	Robert L. Crippen	American

HISTORIC PLACES

ACROPOLIS - The center of Athens, Greece, rising 200 feet above the city. In the fourth century B.C., the Parthenon, a temple, was built there to honor Athena, the patron goddess of Athens.

BERLIN WALL - A wall dividing the city of Berlin into East and West which left little or no communication between inhabitants on both sides. The wall came down in 1989 with the fall of East Germany's Communist government.

CHURCHES OF LALIBELA - Eleven churches built by Ethiopia's King Lalibela in the capital city, Roha. Stoneworkers cut, carved, and hollowed the churches out of solid rock.

CITY OF JERUSALEM - Almost 4,000 years old, a holy city to the believers of Judaism, Christianity, and Islam.

COLOSSEUM (Flavian Amphitheater) - A fine example of ancient Roman architectural engineering standing in the center of present-day Rome; shaped like a football stadium, it once seated about 45,000.

GREAT PYRAMID - The pyramid of Khufu (Cheops), considered a marvel of building skill. Located on the west bank of the Nile River outside Cairo, Egypt, the pyramid contains more than two million stone blocks which weigh 2 1/2 tons each; stands 450 feet high; its base covers 13 acres.

GREAT SPHINX - In Giza, Egypt, one of the most famous monuments in the world. More than 4,800 years old, 240 feet long, 66 feet high. Its head and body are carved from solid rock, and its paws and legs are built of stone blocks.

GREAT WALL OF CHINA - The largest construction project in history; the wall stretches over 1,500 miles of mountainous countryside and was built to keep out invaders from the north.

HAGIA SOPHIA - The "Church of Holy Wisdom," a magnificent church in the Mediterranean world; designed by Byzantine architects.

KREMLIN, THE - A symbol of the Soviet and Czarist governments, located in Moscow; originally built as a fortress, surrounded by a massive brick wall.

LOUVRE - Built as a castle in Paris, France, in 1200. Today it is one of the most famous art museums in the world.

MACHU PICCHU - The remains of an ancient Incan city in the Andes Mountains in Peru, discovered by American archeologist Hiram Bingham.

PALACE OF VERSAILLES - Built by Louis XIV in the 1600s in Versailles, France. It is more than a half mile long and contains hundreds of rooms. Presently a national museum.

PALENQUE - The ruins of a beautiful Mayan city; overlooks a river valley in southern Mexico.

RUINS OF POMPEII - Ancient city in Italy that disappeared after the eruption of Mt. Vesuvius in A.D. 79. Much of the city has been excavated; visitors see buildings and culture 2,000 years old.

STATUE OF LIBERTY - One of the largest statues ever built; overlooks New York Harbor. It was built by a Frenchman and given to the United States in 1884 as a symbol of friendship and liberty. It stands 151 feet, 1 inch high and weighs 450,000 pounds.

STONEHENGE - On the Salisbury Plains in southern England, great chunks of stone in a rough circle, an impressive and mysterious monument from prehistoric times.

TOWER OF LONDON - A great castle fortress built by Duke William of Normandy, completed in 1078. Served many purposes: royal residence, prison, and fortress. Today it is a museum and famous landmark.

VATICAN CITY - An independent state within Rome located on the west bank of the Tiber River, the dwelling place of the Pope, the governing head of Catholicism.

SEVEN WONDERS
OF
THE WORLD

1. **THE EGYPTIAN PYRAMIDS**
   Oldest of all the wonders, only survivor

2. **THE HANGING GARDENS OF BABYLON**
   Built by King Nebuchadnezzar about 600 B.C.

3. **THE MAUSOLEUM AT HALICARNASSUS**
   A huge tomb designed for a Persian ruler by Greek architects

4. **THE TEMPLE OF ARTEMIS AT EPHESUS**
   Famous for its size and beauty

5. **THE COLOSSUS OF RHODES**
   A bronze statue of 120 feet overlooking the harbor of the island of Rhodes

6. **THE LIGHTHOUSE OF ALEXANDRIA**
   As tall as a 30-story building, stood for 1,500 years until destroyed by an earthquake in the 1300s

7. **THE STATUE OF ZEUS AT OLYMPIA**
   Stood over three stories high, made of gold and ivory

MODERN WORLD LEADERS

Aquino, Corazon

Begin, Menachem

Bush, George

Castro, Fidel

Chiang Kai-shek

Churchill, Winston

Clinton, Bill

de Gaulle, Charles

de Klerk, F. W.

Eisenhower, Dwight D.

Emperor Akihito

Gandhi, Mohandas K.

Gorbachev, Mikhail

Hitler, Adolf

Ho Chi Minh

Hussein, Saddam

Kennedy, John F.

Khomeini, Ayatollah Ruhollah

King Fahd

King Hussein

King, Martin Luther, Jr.

Kohl, Helmut

Krushchev, Nikita

Li Peng

Major, John

Mandela, Nelson

Mitterand, Francois

Mubarak, Hosni

Mulroney, Brian

Mussolini, Benito

Nasser, Gamal Abdel

Nixon, Richard

Pope John Paul II

Queen Elizabeth II

Rabin, Yitzhak

Reagan, Ronald

Roosevelt, Franklin D.

Roosevelt, Theodore

el-Sadat, Anwar

Selassie, Haile

Stalin, Joseph

Thatcher, Margaret

Truman, Harry

Tutu, Desmond

Waldheim, Kurt

Xiaoping, Deng

Yang Shangkun

Yeltsin, Boris

Zedong, Mao

BIOGRAPHICAL DICTIONARY

AKBAR (1542-1605): Indian ruler, expanded Mogul Empire

AKHENATON (1375-58 B.C.): Egyptian pharaoh, religious reformer

ALEXANDER II (1818-1881): Russian czar, abolished serfdom

ALEXANDER THE GREAT (356-323 B.C.): Conqueror of Greece and ancient Middle East

AQUINAS, THOMAS (1225?-1274): Dominican monk, Scholastic philosopher

AQUINO, CORAZON (1933-): President of the Philippines

ARISTOTLE (384-322 B.C.): Greek philosopher

ASHURBANIPAL (669-626 B.C.): Ruler of Assyrian Empire

ATTILA (406?-453): King of the Huns, attempted to conquer Rome

AUGUSTINE (354-430): Early Christian thinker

AUGUSTUS (63 B.C.-A.D. 14): First Roman emperor

BACON, FRANCIS (1561-1626): English politician and writer

BEETHOVEN, LUDWIG VAN (1770-1827): German composer

BEGIN, MENACHEM (1913-): Israeli prime minister, signed the Camp David Peace Accords

BISMARCK, OTTO VON (1815-1898): Prussian prime minister, Germany's first chancellor

BOLIVAR, SIMON (1783-1830): Venezuelan leader, drove Spanish out of northern South America

BRAHMS, JOHANNES (1833-1897): German composer

BUSH, GEORGE (1924-): 41st U.S. President

CAESAR, JULIUS (100-44 B.C.): Roman general, statesman, historian

CALVIN, JOHN (1509-1564): French-born Swiss Protestant reformer, developed Calvinism

CASTRO, FIDEL (1927-): Cuban Marxist leader

CATHERINE THE GREAT (1729-1796): Russian ruler

CERVANTES SAAVEDRA, MIGUEL (1547-1616): Spanish author

CHAMPLAIN, SAMUEL DE (1567?-1636): French explorer of eastern Canada

CHARLEMAGNE (724-814): Frankish king, spread Christianity in Europe

CHARLES I (1600-1649): English king, beheaded for treason

CHARLES V (1500-1558): Holy Roman Emperor, ruler of Spain, the Netherlands, and eastern Hapsburg lands

CHAUCER, GEOFFREY (1340?-1400): English author

CHIANG KAI-SHEK (1887-1975): Leader of the Chinese Nationalists

CHURCHILL, WINSTON (1874-1965): British prime minister during World War II

COLUMBUS, CHRISTOPHER (1451?-1506): Italian navigator, discovered the Americas

CONFUCIUS (551-479 B.C.): Chinese philosopher

CONSTANTINE (280?-337): Roman emperor, founded Constantinople

COPERNICUS, NICOLAUS (1473-1543): Polish astronomer whose heliocentric theory claimed the sun was at the center of the universe

CORTES, HERNANDO (1485-1547): Spanish conquistador, defeated Aztecs in Mexico

CROMWELL, OLIVER (1599-1658): Puritan general, overthrew English monarchy and formed the Commonwealth

CURIE, MARIE (1867-1934): and PIERRE (1859-1906): Husband and wife scientists, studied radioactivity in minerals

DANTE ALIGHIERI (1265-1321): Italian author

DARWIN, CHARLES (1809-1882): English scientist, developed theory of evolution

DE GAULLE, CHARLES (1890-1970): Leader of the Free French and president of France's Fifth Republic

DENG XIAOPING (1904-): Chinese leader, succeeded Mao Zedong, started economic reforms

DIAS, BARTHOLOMEU (1450?-1500): Portuguese navigator, discovered Cape of Good Hope

DICKENS, CHARLES (1812-1870): English author

DIOCLETIAN (245-313): Roman emperor

DISRAELI, BENJAMIN (1840-1881): English prime minister, head of Conservative Party

DRAKE, FRANCIS (1540?-1596): English naval hero

EDISON, THOMAS ALVA (1847-1931): American inventor of the electric bulb and the phonograph

EINSTEIN, ALBERT (1879-1955): German-born scientist, developed theory of relativity

EISENHOWER, DWIGHT D. (1890-1969): Leader of Allied forces in World War II, 34th U.S. President

ELEANOR OF AQUITAINE (1122?-1204): Ruler of Aquitaine, wife of Louis VII of France and later of Henry II of England

ELIZABETH I (1533-1603): English queen of the Tudor Dynasty

FRANCIS FERDINAND (1863-1914): Heir to the Austrian-Hungarian throne whose assassination started World War I

FRANCO, FRANCISCO (1892-1975): Spanish Fascist dictator

GALILEO GALILEI (1564-1642): Italian scientist and mathematician, supported Copernicus' heliocentric theory

GANDHI, INDIRA (1917-1984): Prime minister of India

GANDHI, MOHANDAS K. (1869-1948): Indian leader, campaigned for India's independence

GARIBALDI, GIUSEPPE (1807-1882): Commander of the Red Shirts, a group of Italian patriots

GLADSTONE, WILLIAM (1809-1898): English prime minister, head of the Liberal Party

GORBACHEV, MIKHAIL (1931-): Soviet leader, instituted a series of political and economic reforms

GUTENBERG, JOHANN (1398-1468): German printer, produced the first printed book using movable type

HAILE SELASSIE (1892-1975): Ethiopian emperor

HAMMURABI (18th century B.C.): Babylonian ruler, developed a strict code of laws

HANNIBAL (247-183? B.C.): Carthaginian general, led successful attack against the Romans during the Second Punic War

HATSHEPSUT (1504-1482 B.C.): Egyptian queen

HENRY IV (1553-1610): French king, first ruler of Bourbon Dynasty

HENRY VII (1457-1509): English king, founder of Tudor Dynasty

HENRY VIII (1491-1547): English Tudor king

HENRY THE NAVIGATOR (1394-1460): Portuguese prince, sponsored exploration of the West African coast

HERODOTUS (484?-425? B.C.): Greek historian, known as "the father of history"

HITLER, ADOLF (1889-1945): German Nazi dictator

HOBBES, THOMAS (1588-1679): English philosopher and author

HO CHI MINH (1890-1969): Vietnamese Communist leader

HOMER (8th century B.C.): Greek epic poet

HUSS, JOHN (1374-1415): Bohemian religious reformer

HUSSEIN, SADDAM (1937-): Dictator of Iraq, invaded Kuwait in 1990

INNOCENT III (1161-1216): Pope who claimed the right to intervene in the affairs of any European state

ISABELLA (1451-1504): Spanish queen, sponsored Columbus' voyages

IVAN III (1440-1505): Founder of Unified Russia, known as "the Great"

IVAN IV (1530-1584): Russian czar, nicknamed "the Terrible"

JEFFERSON, THOMAS (1743-1826): 3rd U.S. President and author of the Declaration of Independence

JENNER, EDWARD (1749-1823): English doctor, developed vaccine for smallpox

JESUS (4? B.C.-A.D. 29?): One of the world's great religious leaders; believed by most Christians to be the Son of God

JOAN OF ARC (1412-1431): French military heroine

JOHN (1167?-1216): Early English king, signed the Magna Carta

JOHN PAUL II (1920-): Polish pope, encouraged the struggle for religious and political freedom in Communist countries

JOHNSON, LYNDON B. (1908-1973): 36th U.S. President

JUAREZ, BENITO (1806-1872): Mexican reformer and president

JUSTINIAN (482-565): Byzantine ruler

KEATS, JOHN (1795-1821): English Romantic poet

KEMAL, MUSTAFA (1881-1938): First president of the republic of Turkey

KENNEDY, JOHN F. (1917-1963): 35th U.S. President

KENYATTA, JOMO (1894?-1978): Leader of Kenya's independence movement and Kenya's first president

KERENSKY, ALEXANDER (1881-1970): Leader of the Provisional Government set up in Russia in 1917

KHOMEINI, AYATOLLAH RUHOLLAH (1900-1989): Shiite religious leader, headed Iran's government after the overthrow of the shah in 1979

KHRUSHCHEV, NIKITA (1894-1971): Soviet leader from 1953-1964

KING, MARTIN LUTHER, JR. (1929-1968): American civil rights leader

KOHL, HELMUT (1930-): West German chancellor, became chancellor of reunited Germany in 1990

KUBLAI KHAN (1215-1294): Mongol emperor

LAVOISIER, ANTOINE (1743-1794): French chemist, named oxygen

LENIN, VLADIMIR ILYICH (1870-1924): Bolshevik leader, seized control of Russia in 1917

LEONARDO DA VINCI (1452-1519): Italian Renaissance painter, engineer, scientist, and inventor

LINCOLN, ABRAHAM (1809-1865): 16th U.S. President, held office during the Civil War

LISTER, JOSEPH (1827-1912): English surgeon, began use of antiseptics in hospital operating rooms

LOCKE, JOHN (1632-1704): English political philosopher

LOUIS XIV (1638-1715): French ruler, called the "Sun King"

LOUIS XVI (1754-1793): French king whose demand for high taxes began the French Revolution

LOUIS NAPOLEON (1808-1873): French president, became Emperor Napoleon III

LOUIS PHILIPPE (1773-1850): French king known as "Citizen King"

LOYOLA, IGNATIUS (1491-1556): Spanish nobleman, founded Society of Jesuits

LUTHER, MARTIN (1483-1546): German monk, Protestant religious reformer

MACARTHUR, DOUGLAS (1880-1964): American general in WorldWar II

MACHIAVELLI, NICCOLO (1469-1527): Florentine diplomat

MAGELLAN, FERDINAND (1480?-1521): Portuguese navigator whose fleet of ships were the first to circumnavigate the globe

MALTHUS, THOMAS (1766-1834): English economist and minister

MANDELA, NELSON (1918-): Head of the African National Congress in South Africa; imprisoned from 1964-1990

MAO ZEDONG (1893-1976): Chinese Communist leader, formed the People's Republic of China

MARIE ANTOINETTE (1755-1793): French queen, wife of Louis XVI

MARX, KARL (1818-1883): German political philosopher and economist whose theories laid the basis for communism

MENDEL, GREGOR (1822-1884): Austrain monk whose experiments laid the foundation for the science of genetics

MENDELEEV, DMITRI (1834-1907): Russian chemist, classified elements according to their atomic structure

MENES: Egyptian pharaoh, established first dynasty in 3100s B.C.

METTERNICH, KLEMENS VON (1773-1859): Austrian prince and delegate at the Congress of Vienna

MICHELANGELO (1475-1564): Italian Renaissance sculptor, painter, architect, and poet

MITTERAND, FRANCOIS (1916-): French socialist president

MOHAMMED (570?-632): Founder of Islam

MONET, CLAUDE (1840-1926): French impressionist painter

MONTEZUMA (1480?-1520): Aztec ruler of Mexico

MORE, THOMAS (1478-1535): English statesman

MOSES (13th century B.C.): Hebrew prophet and lawgiver

MOZART, WOLFGANG AMADEUS (1756-1791): Austrian composer

MUSSOLINI, BENITO (1883-1945): Italian Fascist leader; dictator of Italy from 1922-1945

NAPOLEON BONAPARTE (1769-1821): French general; overthrew the Directory in 1799 and declared himself emperor in 1804; exiled to St. Helena in 1815

NASSER, GAMAL ABDEL (1918-1970): Egyptian leader

NEBUCHADNEZZAR (630?-562 B.C.): King of Babylon, conquered much of the Fertile Crescent

NEWTON,ISAAC (1642-1727): English mathematician and scientist, showed that all objects in universe obey same laws of motion

NICHOLAS II (1868-1918): Last Russian czar

NIXON, RICHARD M. (1913-): 37th U.S. President and first to resign from office

NKRUMAH, KWAME (1909-1972): Leader of the Gold Coast's independence movement

PAHLAVI, MOHAMMED REZA (1919-1980): Iranian shah, overthrown by Ayatollah Ruhollah Khomeini

PASTEUR, LOUIS (1822-1895): French chemist, discovered that bacteria caused many diseases

PAUL (A.D.5?-67?): Early Christian missionary who developed many of the ideas that form the basis of Christianity

PAVLOV, IVAN (1849-1936): Russian scientist

PERICLES (495?-429 B.C.): Leader of Athens during its "golden age"

PERON, JUAN (1895-1974): Former president of Argentina

PETER THE GREAT (1672-1725): Czar, began to westernize Russia

PETRARCH, FRANCESCO (1304-1374): Italian poet

PHILIP II (1527-1598): Spanish king, worked to expand the power of both Spain and the Roman Catholic Church

PICASSO, PABLO (1881-1973): Spanish painter

PIZARRO, FRANCISCO (1470?-1541): Spanish explorer, defeated the Incas in Peru

PLATO (427-347 B.C.): Greek philosopher

POLO, MARCO (1254?-1325?): Venetian trader whose accounts of his travels stimulated European interest in China

RAMESES II: Egyptian pharaoh (1304-1237 B.C.), ruled during the Hebrews' exodus from Egypt

RASPUTIN (1871?-1916): Self-described holy man, advised Russian czarina Alexandra

REAGAN, RONALD (1911-): 40th U.S. President

RENOIR, PIERRE-AUGUSTE (1841-1919): French impressionist painter

RHODES, CECIL (1853-1902): Englishman who expanded British South African rule into the Rhodesias

RICHELIEU (1585-1642): Chief minister to France's Louis XIII

ROBESPIERRE, MAXIMILIEN (1758-1794): French Jacobin responsible for the Reign of Terror

ROMMEL, ERWIN (1891-1944): German commander of the Nazi Afrika Corps in North Africa during World War II

ROOSEVELT, FRANKLIN D. (1882-1945): 32nd U.S. President, held office during the Great Depression and World War II

ROOSEVELT, THEODORE (1858-1919): 26th U.S. President

ROUSSEAU, JEAN JACQUES (1712-1778): French philosopher, writer

SADAT, ANWAR EL- (1918-1981): Egyptian president, signed the Camp David Peace Accords

SARGON THE GREAT: Ruler of Akkad in 3200s B.C., created the world's first empire

SAUD, IBN (1880-1953): Saudi Arabian king

SHAKESPEARE, WILLIAM (1564-1616): English poet and playwright

SHAW, GEORGE BERNARD (1856-1950): Irish-born English playwright

SHOTOKU (6th century A.D.): Japanese prince and author of the Seventeen-Article Constitution

SIDDHARTHA GAUTAMA (563?-483?): Founder of Buddhism

SMITH, ADAM (1723-1790): Scottish economist

SOCRATES (470?-300 B.C.): Greek philosopher

SOPHOCLES (496?-406 B.C.): Greek dramatist

STALIN, JOSEPH (1879-1953): Communist leader, followed Lenin as ruler of the Soviet Union; ruled as totalitarian dictator through the 1930s and World War II

SULEIMAN I (1490?-1566): Sultan of the Ottoman Empire

SUN YAT-SEN (1866-1925): Leader of Nationalist Revolution in China

THATCHER, MARGARET (1925-): First woman prime minister of Britain

THUCYDIDES (471-400 B.C.): Greek historian

TOKUGAWA IEYASU (17th-century A.D.): Japanese ruler, established the last shogunate to rule Japan

TOLSTOY, LEO (1828-1910): Russian author

TOUSSAINT L'OUVERTURE, PIERRE (1743-1803): Haitian revolutionary and statesman

TROTSKY, LEON (1879-1940): Bolshevik leader

TRUMAN, HARRY (1884-1972): 33rd U.S. President

TUTU, DESMOND (1931-): South African archbishop, won the Nobel Peace Prize in 1984 for his work against apartheid

VAN GOGH, VINCENT (1853-1890): Dutch post-impressionist painter

VENERABLE BEDE (673-735): English monk, completed a history of the Church in England

VERDI, GIUSEPPE (1813-1901): Italian composer

VIRGIL (70-19 B.C.): Roman who wrote the *Aeneid*

VLADIMIR (965?-1015): Kievan prince, brought Christianity to Russia

VOLTAIRE (1694-1778): French philosopher and writer

WALESA, LECH (1943?-): Polish labor leader and president

WASHINGTON, GEORGE (1732-1799): Commander of the Continental Army and the first U.S. President

WILLIAM II (1859-1941): German kaiser, gave up his throne when Germany was defeated in World War I

WILLIAM THE CONQUEROR (1027-1087): Duke of Normandy, defeated the Saxons at the Battle of Hastings and then became king of England

WILSON, WOODROW (1856-1924): 28th U.S. President

WU HOU (690-735): Chinese empress and the only woman in China to rule in her own right

WYCLIFFE, JOHN (1320?-1384): Religious reformer, completed the first English translation of the Bible

GLOSSARY OF TERMS #1

ABDICATE: to give up a powerful position, especially a throne

ABSOLUTE MONARCHY: a government in which a ruler has complete power

AGE OF EXPLORATION: the period (about 1450-1700) when European sea captains made voyages of exploration; expanded European power around the world

AGORA: the marketplace of an ancient Greek city

AHIMSA: a Buddhist doctrine of nonviolence; stresses the sacredness of human and animal life

ALCHEMY: an ancient field of study based on searching for ways to turn common metals into gold

ALLIES: the countries that allied against the Central Powers during World War I, including France, Britain, and Russia; the countries that allied against Axis Powers during World War II

ANNEX: to add territory to an existing country

APARTHEID: South Africa's government policy of racial segregation and white supremacy

AQUEDUCT: a bridgelike structure supporting a channel through which water is transported over a distance

ARCHIPELAGO: a large group of islands

ARCHON: one of a group of officials, chosen from the nobility, who ruled Athens before Solon's political reforms

ARMAMENTS: weapons and military supplies

ARMISTICE: a halt to fighting; a truce

ARTIFACT: an object, made by a human being in the distant past, that has survived to the present

ARTISAN: a worker with skill in a specific craft

AUTOCRAT: a ruler with unlimited power

AXIS POWERS: the alliance of Germany, Italy, and Japan in World War II

BALANCE OF POWER: the distribution of power among nations so that no one country dominates

BARON: a feudal lord

BARTER: a form of trade in which people exchange goods without using money

BLITZKRIEG: a German word meaning "lightning war"; a sudden, rapid military attack

BLOC: a group of nations, parties, or people united for a common purpose

BOURGEOISIE: the middle class

BRONZE AGE: the period when bronze replaced copper and stone as the main material used in tools and weapons

BUREAUCRAT: a trained public official who is appointed, not elected

CALIPH: a Muslim political and religious leader

CARBON 14 DATING: analysis of the amount of carbon 14 within a once-living material, used to determine approximate age

CASTE: in Hindu society, a fixed social grouping based on class, occupation, and tradition

CHARTER: a document granting a group of people certain rights and privileges

CHIVALRY: a code of behavior for feudal knights and nobles

CIRCUMNAVIGATE: to go completely around something

CIRCUS MAXIMUS: a Roman outdoor arena in which public games, such as chariot races, were held

CITY-STATE: an independent, self-governing community consisting of a city and the surrounding territory

CIVIL DISOBEDIENCE: the use of nonviolent resistance to defy laws thought to be unjust

CIVILIZATION: an advanced level of culture, usually characterized by organized government and religion, division of labor, a class structure, and a system of writing

CIVIL RIGHTS: the right to be treated equally under the law and have equality of opportunity

CLAN: a group of families or a small tribal community

CLASSICAL: a style of art and thought emphasizing order and simplicity

CODE OF HAMMURABI: the laws of Hammurabi, 1700s B.C. King of Babylon, carved on a block of stone

COLD WAR: the term applied to the period of extreme tension and hostility between the U.S. and the Soviet Union in the years following World War II

CULTURE: the unique way of life of a people

CUNEIFORM: system of writing used by Sumerians and later peoples in Mesopotamia, with wedge-shaped characters marked on clay tablets

CZAR: the title given to Russian emperors from the late 1400s to 1918

DEMOCRACY: a form of government based on rule by the people

DEPOSE: to remove a person from a throne or other high office

DETENTE: a relaxing of tensions between nations

DHARMA: the rights and duties of members of various classes in Indian society

DICTATOR: a ruler with absolute power

DIVINE RIGHT: the theory that monarchs receive their power from God, and that a monarch's power should not be questioned or disobeyed

DYNASTY: a series of rulers from the same family

EMBARGO: a suspension of foreign trade, often limited to certain products and directed at a specific region

EXCAVATE: to dig up an archeological site

FASCISM: an ideology that stresses nationalism and dictatorship and places the strength of the state above the welfare of individual citizens

FEUDALISM: a political system in which a king granted the use of land to nobles in return for loyalty, military assistance, and services

FIVE PILLARS OF ISLAM: the five religious duties of Muslims, including prayer, fasting, and pilgrimages to the holy city of Mecca

FOUR NOBLE TRUTHS: the major principles of Buddhism

FOURTEEN POINTS: President WoodrowWilson's terms for peace after World War I

GLACIER: a huge, slow-moving sheet of ice

GLADIATOR: a person, usually a slave or condemned criminal, who fought other gladiators or wild animals as public entertainment in ancient Rome

GLASNOST: beginning under Gorbachev in the 1980s, a government policy of openness about problems within the Soviet Union

GREAT WALL: a 1,500-mile stone wall stretching across northern China

GUILD: medieval organization formed by merchants of the same trade to protect its members and set business policies

HAGIA SOPHIA: a cathedral built in Constantinople (532-537), featuring a dome over a rectangular building

HEGIRA: Mohamamed's flight from Mecca to Medina in 622

HELIOCENTRIC THEORY: the belief that the sun is the center of the universe

HIEROGLYPHICS: ancient Egyptian writing

HISTORY: the study of the human past; a record of events and developments from the past

HOLOCAUST: the Nazi plan for the systematic murder of European Jews

HOME RULE: the policy of giving one part of an empire local control over its internal matters

HUMAN RIGHTS: basic rights and freedoms to which all people are entitled

ICE AGE: one of the extremely long periods during which temperatures in the Northern Hemisphere were cold enough to produce huge sheets of ice over much of the land

IMPERIAL: relating to an empire or emperor

IRON AGE: the period following the Bronze Age when knowledge of ironworking spread

KARMA: in Hinduism, the accumulated good and bad acts of all of one's previous lives

KNIGHT: a mounted warrior in medieval Europe

KREMLIN: a palace-fortress in Moscow where Bolsheviks set up the government after their takeover

LEAGUE OF NATIONS: an organization of nations established in 1920 to promote world peace

MAGINOT LINE: a string of heavily defended forts built by France along its border with Germany in the 1930s

MARTIAL LAW: strict controls maintained over a nation by military forces

MEDIEVAL: relating to the Middle Ages

MIDDLE AGES: the period from about A.D. 500 to 1500 that began with the decline of the Roman Empire

MIGRATE: to move from one region or country and settle in another

NATO: the North Atlantic Treaty Organization

NEW STONE AGE: the part of the Stone Age that began about 8000 B.C. with the development of farming; also called Neolithic Age

NIRVANA: the Buddhist term for a state of enlightenment

NOMAD: one of a group who has no fixed home and wanders from place to place in search of food and water

OLD STONE AGE: the earliest and longest part of the Stone Age, which began more than two million years ago; also called the Paleolithic Age

OPEC: the Organization of Petroleum Exporting Countries

ORACLE: a temple where priests and priestesses in ancient Greece gave prophecies; also the priest or priestess giving the prophecy

PAPACY: the office or authority of the Pope

PARTHENON: the temple of Athena, which stands on the Acropolis in Athens

POLIS: a city-state of ancient Greece

PREHISTORY: the period of time before writing and other record-keeping systems were developed

REFORMATION: the sixteenth-century European movement that rebelled against the authority of the Roman Catholic Church

RENAISSANCE: meaning "rebirth," the period of Western history, beginning in the 1300s, when far-reaching changes occurred in the arts, in intellectual life, and in ways of viewing the world

REPARATIONS: payments made by one nation to another in compensation for property destroyed in war

REPUBLIC: in ancient Rome, a form of government that was not a monarchy; in modern times, a democratic government

RESTORATION: the period (1660-1685) following the English Civil War, during which Charles II reigned in England

ROMANTICISM: a nineteenth-century movement that stressed emotion and imagination over order and reason and that influenced European social and political thinking, art, and literature

SAMURAI: a class of noble warriors in feudal Japan

SAVANNA: a flat, open grassland with scattered clumps of trees and shrubs

SERF: a medieval peasant legally bound to live and work on a lord's estate

SHAH: a Muslim ruler

SILK ROAD: in ancient China, the route that silk merchants traveled as they headed westward

SOCIALISM: a philosophy that calls for government or worker ownership and operation of business and industry for the benefit of society

STONE AGE: the name for the prehistoric period when tools and weapons were made of stone

STURM UND DRANG: meaning "storm and stress"; a literary movement formed in the 1770s by German writers emphasizing the individual, emotion, and the imagination.

SUFFRAGE: the right to vote

SUMMIT: a meeting between top government officials from two or more countries

TAJ MAHAL: a tomb in Agra built by Shah Jahan for his wife; considered a masterpiece of Mogul architecture

TECHNOLOGY: the development of methods, materials, and tools used in doing work

THEOCRACY: a form of government in which the ruler is seen either as a god or as a chosen representative of the gods

URBANIZATION: the movement of people from rural areas to cities

UTOPIA: an ideal society

VATICAN: the palace of the Pope in Rome

VERSAILLES: a palace in France built as the home for Louis XIV

◼◼◼◼◼◼◼ WORLD GEOGRAPHY ◼◼◼◼◼◼◼

LAND AND SEA

CONTINENTS

AFRICA (11,684,000 square miles)

ANTARCTICA (5,400,000 square miles)

ASIA (16,989,000 square miles)

AUSTRALIA (2,966,000 square miles)

EUROPE (4,065,000 square miles)

NORTH AMERICA (9,360,000 square miles)

SOUTH AMERICA (6,887,500 square miles)

OCEANS

ARCTIC OCEAN

ATLANTIC OCEAN

INDIAN OCEAN

PACIFIC OCEAN

MAJOR ISLANDS

BAFFIN	JAPAN
BRITISH ISLES	MADAGASCAR
CUBA	NEW GUINEA
GREENLAND	NEW ZEALAND
HONSU	NEWFOUNDLAND
ICELAND	PHILIPPINES
INDONESIA	VICTORIA

GULFS AND SEAS

BALTIC SEA	MEDITERRANEAN SEA
BERING SEA	NORTH SEA
BLACK SEA	PERSIAN GULF
CARIBBEAN SEA	RED SEA
EAST CHINA SEA	SEA OF JAPAN
GULF OF CALIFORNIA	SOUTH CHINA SEA
GULF OF MEXICO	YELLOW SEA

CLIMATIC REGIONS

MAJOR CLIMATE ZONES

Tropics (Low Latitudes)
The area between the Tropic of Cancer and the Tropic of Capricorn; this is the warmest part of the earth.
 Average Temperature - 79°F (26°C) Hot all year
 Average Precipitation - Yearly: 100 in. (254 cm.)
 Monthly: 8.3 in. (21 cm.)

Middle Latitudes
The area between the Tropic of Cancer and the Arctic Circle, and the area between the Tropic of Capricorn and the Antarctic Circle; this is the temperate zone. The summers are warm and the winters are cold.
 Dry - Semiarid: hot summers, mild to cold winters
 Average Temperature - Summer: 78°F (26°C) Winter: 51°F (11°C)
 Average Precipitation - Yearly: 18 in. (46 cm.)
  Monthly: Summer 3.4 in. (7 cm.) Winter: 0.2 in. (0.5 cm.)
 Dry - Arid: hot days, cold nights
 Average Temperature - Summer: 81°F (26°C) Winter: 55°F (13°C)
 Average Precipitation - Yearly: 5 in. (13 cm.)
  Monthly: Summer 0.6 in. (7 cm.) Winter: 0.1 in. (0.2 cm.)
 Humid Subtropical: hot summers, cool winters
 Average Temperature - Summer: 77°F (25°C) Winter: 47°F (8°C)
 Average Precipitation - Yearly: 50 in. (127 cm.)
  Monthly: Summer 6.2 in. (16 cm.) Winter: 2.6 in. (7 cm.)
 Marine West Coast: warm summers, cool winters
 Average Temperature - Summer: 60°F (16°C) Winter: 42°F (6°C)
 Average Precipitation - Yearly: 45 in. (114 cm.)
  Monthly: Summer 2.6 in. (6 cm.) Winter: 5.5 in. (14 cm.)
 Continental: warm summers, cool winters
 Average Temperature - Summer: 66°F (16°C) Winter: 21°F (-6°C)
 Average Precipitation - Yearly: 27 in. (67 cm.)
  Monthly: Summer: 3.2 in. (8 cm.) Winter: 1.6 in. (4 cm.)
 Subarctic: cool summers, very cold winters
 Average Temperature - Summer: 56°F (13°C) Winter: -8°F (-22°C)
 Average Precipitation - Yearly: 17 in. (43 cm.)
  Monthly: Summer: 1.8 in. (15 cm.) Winter: 1.2 in. (3 cm.)

Polar Regions (High Latitudes)
The high latitudes closest to the North Pole and the South Pole. These are the coldest areas on earth.
 Average Temperature - Summer: 40°F (4°C) Winter: 0°F (-18°C)
 Average Precipitation - Yearly: 16 in. (41 cm.)
  Monthly: Summer: 1.9 in. (5 cm.) Winter: 1.2 in. (3 cm.)

THE NATIONS OF THE WORLD

NATION	CAPITAL	AREA (sq. mi.)	POPULATION
AFRICA			
Algeria	Algiers	919,595	25,600,000
Angola	Luanda	481,350	8,500,000
Benin	Porto-Novo	43,483	4,700,000
Botswana	Gaborone	231,800	1,200,000
Burkina Faso	Ouagadougou	105,870	9,100,000
Burundi	Bujumbura	10,747	5,600,000
Cameroon	Yaounde	183,569	11,100,000
Cape Verde	Praia	1,557	400,000
Central African Republic	Bangui	241,313	2,900,000
Chad	N'Djamena	495,752	5,000,000
Comoros	Moroni	690	500,000
Congo	Brazzaville	132,046	2,200,000
Djibouti	Djibouti	8,490	400,000
Egypt	Cairo	386,900	54,700,000
Equatorial Guinea	Malabo	10,830	400,000
Ethiopia	Addis Ababa	472,432	51,700,000
Gabon	Libreville	103,346	1,200,000
Gambia	Banjul	4,093	900,000
Ghana	Accra	92,100	15,000,000
Guinea	Conakry	94,925	7,300,000
Guinea-Bissau	Bissau	13,948	1,000,000
Ivory Coast	Abidjan	124,502	12,600,000
Kenya	Nairobi	224,960	24,600,000
Lesotho	Maseru	11,720	1,800,000
Liberia	Monrovia	43,000	2,600,000
Libya	Tripoli	679,536	4,200,000
Madagascar	Antananarivo	226,660	12,000,000
Malawi	Lilongwe	45,747	9,200,000
Mali	Bamako	478,819	8,100,000
Mauritania	Nouakchott	397,953	2,000,000
Mauritius	Port Louis	787	1,100,000
Morocco	Rabat	172,413	25,600,000
Mozambique	Maputo	303,073	15,700,000
Namibia	Windhoek	318,261	1,500,000
Niger	Niamey	489,206	7,900,000
Nigeria	Lagos	356,700	118,800,000
Rwanda	Kigali	10,169	7,300,000
Sao Tome & Principe	Sao Tome	370	100,000
Senegal	Dakar	75,954	7,400,000
Seychelles	Victoria	175	100,000
Sierra Leone	Freetown	27,700	4,200,000
Somalia	Mogadishu	246,199	8,400,000
South Africa	Pretoria, Cape Town	471,440	39,600,000
Sudan	Khartoum	967,491	25,200,000

NATION	CAPITAL	AREA *(sq. mi.)*	POPULATION
Swaziland	Mbabane	6,704	800,000
Tanzania	Dar es Salaam	364,900	26,000,000
Togo	Lome	21,925	3,700,000
Tunisia	Tunis	63,379	8,100,000
Uganda	Kampala	91,343	18,000,000
Zaire	Kinshasa	905,365	36,600,000
Zambia	Lusaka	290,586	8,100,000
Zimbabwe	Harare	150,699	9,700,000

THE AMERICAS

NATION	CAPITAL	AREA *(sq. mi.)*	POPULATION
Antigua & Barbuda	St. John's	170	100,000
Argentina	Buenos Aires	1,072,067	32,300,000
Bahamas	Nassau	5,380	200,000
Barbados	Bridgetown	166	300,000
Belize	Belmopan	8,867	200,000
Bolivia	La Paz, Sucre	424,162	7,300,000
Brazil	Brasilia	286,470	150,400,000
Canada	Ottawa	3,851,809	26,600,000
Chile	Santiago	292,132	13,200,000
Colombia	Bogota	455,355	31,800,000
Costa Rica	San Jose	19,652	3,000,000
Cuba	Havana	44,218	10,600,000
Dominica	Roseau	290	100,000
Dominican Republic	Santo Domingo	18,704	7,200,000
Ecuador	Quito	109,484	10,700,000
El Salvador	San Salvador	8,260	5,300,000
Grenada	St. George's	133	100,000
Guatemala	Guatemala City	42,042	9,200,000
Guyana	Georgetown	83,000	800,000
Haiti	Port-au-Prince	10,714	6,500,000
Honduras	Tegucigalpa	43,277	5,100,000
Jamaica	Kingston	4,411	2,400,000
Mexico	Mexico City	761,600	88,600,000
Nicaraugua	Managua	50,180	3,900,000
Panama	Panama City	29,761	2,400,000
Paraguay	Asuncion	157,047	4,300,000
Peru	Lima	496,222	21,900,000
St. Kitts	Basseterre	100	40,000
St. Lucia	Castries	238	200,000
St. Vincent & the Grenadines	Kingstown	150	100,000
Suriname	Paramaribo	63,251	400,000
Trinidad & Tobago	Port-of-Spain	1,980	1,300,000
United States	Washington, D.C.	3,540,939	251,400,000
Uruguay	Montevideo	68,040	3,000,000
Venezuela	Caracas	352,143	19,600,000

NATION	CAPITAL	AREA *(sq. mi.)*	POPULATION
ASIA			
Afghanistan	Kabul	250,000	15,900,000
Azerbaijan	Baku	33,400	7,000,000
Bangladesh	Dhaka	55,598	114,800,000
Bhutan	Thimpu	18,000	1,600,000
Brunei	Bandar Seri Begawan	2,226	300,000
Burma (Myanmar)	Rangoon	261,220	41,300,000
Cambodia	Phnom Penh	69,884	7,000,000
China	Beijing	3,691,521	1,119,900,000
India	New Delhi	1,229,737	853,400,000
Indonesia	Jakarta	735,268	189,400,000
Japan	Tokyo	143,574	123,600,000
Kazakhstan	Alma-ata	1,049,200	16,500,000
North Korea	Pyongyang	46,768	21,300,000
South Korea	Seoul	38,031	42,800,000
Kyrgyzstan	Frunze	76,642	4,300,000
Laos	Vientiane	91,429	4,000,000
Malaysia	Kuala Lumpur	128,328	17,900,000
Maldives	Male	115	200,000
Mongolia	Ulan Bator	604,250	2,200,000
Nepal	Kathmandu	54,463	19,100,000
Pakistan	Islamabad	310,400	114,600,000
Philippines	Manila	115,830	66,100,000
Russia	Moscow	6,592,812	147,400,000
Singapore	Singapore	220	2,700,000
Sri Lanka	Colombo	25,332	17,200,000
Taiwan	Taipei	13,895	20,200,000
Tajikistan	Dushanbe	54,019	5,100,000
Thailand	Bangkok	198,455	55,700,000
Turkmenistan	Ashkhabad	188,417	3,500,000
Uzbekistan	Tashkent	172,700	19,900,000
Vietnam	Hanoi	127,246	70,200,000

NATION	CAPITAL	AREA (sq. mi.)	POPULATION
EUROPE			
Albania	Tirana	11,100	3,300,000
Andorra	Andorra la Vella	175	50,000
Armenia	Yerevan	11,306	3,300,000
Austria	Vienna	32,375	7,600,000
Belarus	Minsk	80,200	10,200,000
Belgium	Brussels	11,781	9,900,000
Bosnia and Herzegovina	Sarajevo	19,741	4,651,000
Bulgaria	Sofia	42,823	8,900,000
Croatia	Zagreb	21,829	4,698,000
Cyprus	Nicosia	3,572	700,000
Czech Republic	Prague	30,449	10,408,000
Denmark	Copenhagen	16,631	5,100,000
Estonia	Tallinn	17,413	1,600,000
Finland	Helsinki	130,119	5,000,000
France	Paris	211,208	56,400,000
Georgia	Tbilisi	26,911	5,500,000
Germany	Berlin	137,777	79,500,000
Greece	Athens	50,961	10,100,000
Hungary	Budapest	35,919	10,600,000
Iceland	Reykjavik	39,709	300,000
Ireland	Dublin	26,600	3,500,000
Italy	Rome	116,500	57,700,000
Latvia	Riga	24,695	2,700,000
Liechtenstein	Vaduz	61	28,000
Lithuania	Vilna	26,173	3,700,000
Luxembourg	Luxembourg	999	400,000
Macedonia	Skopje	9,928	2,214,000
Malta	Valletta	122	400,000
Moldova	Kishinev	13,012	4,300,000
Monaco	Monaco-Ville	73	28,000
Netherlands	Amsterdam, The Hague	16,041	14,900,000
Norway	Oslo	125,049	4,200,000
Poland	Warsaw	120,727	37,800,000
Portugal	Lisbon	35,550	10,400,000
Romania	Bucharest	91,700	23,300,000
Russia	Moscow	8,649,489	291,000,000
San Marino	San Marino	24	23,000
Slovakia	Bratislava	18,933	5,404,000
Slovenia	Ljubljana	7,821	1,972,000
Spain	Madrid	194,885	39,400,000
Sweden	Stockholm	173,800	8,500,000
Switzerland	Bern	15,941	6,700,000
Ukraine	Kiev	233,089	51,700,000
United Kingdom	London	94,247	57,400,000

THE NATIONS OF THE WORLD *(cont.)*

NATION	CAPITAL	AREA *(sq. mi.)*	POPULATION
Vatican City	Vatican City	17	800
Yugoslavia (Serbia)	Belgrade	39,449	10,760,000

MIDDLE EAST (NOT INCLUDING NORTH AFRICA)

NATION	CAPITAL	AREA *(sq. mi.)*	POPULATION
Bahrain	Manama	240	500,000
Iran	Tehran	636,293	55,600,000
Iraq	Baghdad	167,920	18,800,000
Israel	Jerusalem	8,020	4,600,000
Jordan	Amman	37,297	4,100,000
Kuwait	Kuwait	6,880	2,100,000
Lebanon	Beirut	4,015	3,300,000
Oman	Muscat	82,030	1,500,000
Qatar	Doha	4,000	500,000
Saudi Arabia	Riyadh	865,000	15,000,000
Syria	Damascus	71,498	12,600,000
Turkey	Ankara	300,947	56,700,000
United Arab Emirates	Abu Dhabi	32,000	1,600,000
Yemen	Sanaa	203,850	9,800,000

OCEANIA

NATION	CAPITAL	AREA *(sq. mi.)*	POPULATION
Australia	Canberra	2,966,150	17,100,000
Fiji	Suva	7,078	800,000
Kiribati	Tarawa	277	69,000
Nauru	Yaren	8	9,100
New Zealand	Wellington	103,884	3,300,000
Papua New Guinea	Port Moresby	178,704	4,000,000
Solomon Islands	Honiara	11,500	300,000
Tonga	Nuku'alofa	290	100,000
Tuvalu	Funafuti	10	9,000
Vanuatu	Port Vila	5,700	200,000
Western Samoa	Apia	1,093	200,000

SIGHTS TO SEE

SIGHT and LOCATION

ACROPOLIS...Athens, Greece

THE ALHAMBRA...Granada, Spain

CALIFORNIA REDWOODS ....Sequoia National Park, California

COLOGNE CATHEDRAL...Cologne, Germany

COLOSSEUM ....Rome, Italy

COLOSSI OF ABU SIMBEL ....Egypt

DUOMO..Rome, Italy

EASTER ISLAND STATUES.......................................Easter Island

EIFFEL TOWER...Paris, France

FORBIDDEN CITY ....Tibet

GOLDEN GATE BRIDGE ....San Francisco, California

GRAND CANAL ....Venice, Italy

GRAND CANYON...Arizona

GREAT BUDDHA OF KAMAKURA (Daibutsu)..............................Japan

GREAT SPHINX...Giza, Egypt

GREAT PYRAMID..Giza, Egypt

GREAT WALL OF CHINA ....China

THE HRADCANY...Prague, Czechoslovakia

THE KA'BA AT MECCA...............................Mecca, Saudi Arabia

KREMLIN...Moscow, Russia

LEANING TOWER OF PISA ....Pisa, Italy

MACHU PICCHU ....Peru

THE MATTERHORN ....Zermatt, Switzerland

MILAN CATHEDRAL...Milan, Italy

MONT ST. MICHEL...France

MONTSERRAT MONASTERY ....Catalonian Mountains, Spain

MOUNT ABU ....India

MOUNT KILIMANJARO ....Kenya, Africa

MOUNT OF OLIVES...Jerusalem, Israel

MOUNT RUSHMORE..................................Black Hills, South Dakota

NIAGARA FALLS ....New York and Canada

NOTRE DAME CATHEDRAL ....Paris, France

OLD FAITHFUL GEYSER...........................Yellowstone National Park

PALACE OF VERSAILLES ....Paris, France

PILLAR OF DELHI...Delhi, India

PLACE DE LA CONCORDE...Paris, France

PUEBLO CLIFF PALACE ....Colorado

RUINS OF POMPEII ....Pompeii, Italy

SOGNE FJORD...Norway

ST. PETER'S CATHEDRAL ....Rome, Italy

STATUE OF LIBERTY ....New York City, New York

STONEHENGE ....Wiltshire, England (Salisbury Plain)

STRASBOURG CATHEDRAL...........................Strasbourg, Germany

TAJ MAHAL ....India

TEMPLE CITY OF ANGKOR ....Cambodia

TEMPLE CITY OF MADURA...India

TEMPLES OF KARNAK AND KOM-OMBO ....Egypt

VICTORIA FALLS ....Rhodesia, Africa

WESTMINSTER ABBEY...................................London, England

WORLD RIVERS

RIVER	LENGTH (miles)	RIVER	LENGTH (miles)
ALBANY	610	NELSON	410
AMAZON	4,000	NIGER	2,590
AMU	1,578	NILE	4,160
AMUR	2,744	OB-IRTYSH	3,362
ANGARA	1,151	ODER	567
ARKANSAS	1,459	OHIO	1,310
BACK	605	ORANGE	1,300
BRAHMAPUTRA	1,800	ORINOCO	1,600
BUG, SOUTHERN	532	OTTAWA	790
BUG, WESTERN	481	PARAGUAY	1,584
CANADIAN	906	PARANA	2,485
CHANG JIANG	3,964	PEACE	1,210
CHURCHILL, Man.	1,000	GPILCOMAYO	1,000
CHURCHILL, Que.	532	PO	405
COLORADO	1,450	PURUS	2,100
COLUMBIA	1,243	RED	1,290
CONGO	2,718	RED RIVER OF N.	545
DANUBE	1,776	RHINE	820
DNIEPER	1,420	RHONE	505
DNIESTER	877	RIO DE LA PLATA	150
DON	1,224	RIO GRANDE	1,900
DRAVA	447	RIO ROOSEVELT	400
DVINA, NORTH	824	SAGUENAY	434
DVINA, WEST	634	ST. JOHN	418
EBRO	565	ST. LAWRENCE	800
ELBE	724	SALWEEN	1,500
EUPHRATES	1,700	SAO FRANCISCO	1,988
FRASER	850	SASKATCHEWAN	1,205
GAMBIA	700	SEINE	496
GANGES	1,560	SHANNON	230
GARONNE	357	SNAKE	1,038
HUANG (YELLOW)	2,903	SONGHUA	1,150
INDUS	1,800	SYR	1,370
IRRAWADDY	1,337	TAJO, TAGUS	626
JAPURA	1,750	TENNESSEE	652
JORDAN	200	THAMES	236
AKOOTENAY	485	TIBER	252
LENA	2,734	TIGRIS	1,180
LOIRE	634	TISZA	600
MACKENZIE	2,635	TOCANTINS	1,677
MADEIRA	2,013	URAL	1,575
MAGDALENA	956	URUGUAY	1,000
MARNE	326	VOLGA	2,194
MEKONG	2,600	WESER	454
MEUSE	580	WISLA	675
MISSISSIPPI	2,340	XI	1,200
MISSOURI	2,540	YENISEY	2,543
MURRAY-DARLING	2,310	YUKON	1,979
NEGRO	1,400	ZAMBEZI	1,700

MAJOR CITIES OF THE WORLD

RANK	NAME	POPULATION
1.	MEXICO CITY	10,061,000
2.	SEOUL	9,645,932
3.	TOKYO	8,353,674
4.	MOSCOW	8,275,000
5.	BOMBAY	8,227,332
6.	NEW YORK CITY	7,071,639
7.	SAO PAULO	7,033,529
8.	SHANGHAI	6,880,000
9.	LONDON	6,767,500
10.	JAKARTA	6,503,449
11.	CAIRO	5,875,000
12.	BEIJING	5,760,000
13.	TEHRAN	5,734,199
14.	HONG KONG	5,659,000
15.	TIANJIN	5,300,000
16.	KARACHI	5,208,170
17.	BANGKOK	5,153,902
18.	RIO DE JANEIRO	5,093,232
19.	DELHI	4,884,234
20.	LENINGRAD	4,295,000
21.	SANTIAGO	4,225,299
22.	LIMA	4,164,597
23.	SHENYANG	4,130,000
24.	BOGOTA	3,982,941
25.	PUSAN	3,516,807
26.	HO CHI MINH CITY	3,419,978
27.	SYDNEY	3,364,858
28.	WUHAN	3,340,000
29.	CALCUTTA	3,305,006
30.	MADRAS	3,276,622
31.	GUANGZHOU	3,220,000
32.	MADRID	3,188,297
33.	BERLIN	3,062,979
34.	CHICAGO	3,005,072
35.	YOKOHAMA	2,992,644
36.	BAGHDAD	2,969,000
37.	LOS ANGELES	2,968,579
38.	LAHORE	2,952,689
39.	BUENOS AIRES	2,908,001
40.	MELBOURNE	2,832,893
41.	ROME	2,830,569
42.	ISTANBUL	2,772,708
43.	CHONGQING	2,730,000
44.	PYONGYANG	2,639,448
45.	OSAKA	2,636,260
46.	HARBIN	2,590,000
47.	HANOI	2,570,905
48.	CHENGDU	2,540,000
49.	BANGALORE	2,476,355
50.	KIEV	2,409,000

GLOSSARY OF TERMS #2

ACROPOLIS: a walled fortress built on a hill

AGRICULTURE: farming

ALTITUDE: height above sea level

ATLAS: a collection of maps

CATHEDRAL: a large church

CENSUS: a population count

CLASS: a group of people making up part of a society

DELTA: a deposit of rich soil at the mouth of a river

ECONOMY: the way people use resources to meet their needs

ELEVATION: height of land above sea level

EMPIRE: a group of peoples and places under one ruler

ENVIRONMENT: surroundings

GEOGRAPHY: the study of the physical features, resources, climate, and people of the earth

INDEX: an alphabetical list of the subjects and their page references in a book

ISTHMUS: a narrow strip of land, with water on both sides, that connects two larger masses of land

LEGEND: a key on a map that explains its features

LINES OF LATITUDE: the imaginary lines that go east and west around the earth; parallels

LINES OF LONGITUDE: the imaginary lines running from the North Pole to the South Pole; meridians

NATURAL RESOURCES: things in nature people can use

OASIS: a fertile place in the desert

PAMPAS: Indian for "plains"; the vast, grassy plains of Argentina

PAPYRUS: reeds that grow in the Nile River Valley, used to make paper

PERIODICAL: a newspaper or magazine

PHARAOH: a ruler of ancient Egypt

POLICY: plan of action

RAIN FOREST: a place with rain almost all year round, where trees and plants grow close together

SOCIETY: a group of people bound by common laws and culture

STEPPES: semidry plains, which produce some grasses and thorny plants

TEMPERATE: having a mild or moderate climate

TIME ZONE: a geographical area within which the same standard time is used

TRADITION: a custom or belief passed from one generation to the next

TROPICS: the low latitudes on the earth where climates are warm most of the year

TUNDRA: cold, treeless plain whose subsoil is permanently frozen

VELD: broad, grassy plains in Southern Africa

WORLD SOCIAL STUDIES YELLOW PAGES FOR STUDENTS AND TEACHERS
from the KIDS' STUFF™ People

Instead of searching through ponderous resources, turn to the WORLD SOCIAL STUDIES YELLOW PAGES FOR STUDENTS AND TEACHERS! It is an amazing time-saving collection of facts, charts, lists, definitions, and resources that will give you a comprehensive bank of World Social Studies information. Within these pages you will find important information on the rise of civilization, classical civilization, medieval civilization, the Renaissance, Reformation, exploration, colonization, revolution, and modern times. Important geographical information includes lists of continents, major regions of the world, rivers, landforms, major cities, plus population and language information. In addition, a biographical dictionary and a glossary of terms are provided. You are sure to discover that this is a Social Studies reference you can't live without!

*Don't miss these other timesaving titles from the **Yellow Pages Series!***

MATH YELLOW PAGES   **ECOLOGY GREEN PAGES**
READING YELLOW PAGES   **U.S. SOCIAL STUDIES YELLOW PAGES**
SCIENCE YELLOW PAGES   **WRITING YELLOW PAGES**

ISBN 0-86530-268-5

90000

9 780865 302686

ISBN 0-86530-268-5

0 29072 02685 5